Christianity and Health & Educational Development in South Travancore

Christian Heritage Rediscovered

The Series, as the name suggests, is meant to focus on Christian Faith & Living vis-à-vis topics like Literature & Poetry, Indigenous Philosophizing, Ethical response towards Agriculture, Health & Healing, Science & Technology, Eco-feminist Theology, Sociological approach towards Human Rights, Law & Politics, Arts, History of Ideas, Ancient Civilizations, Cultural Contiguity, Religious Cosmologies & Mysticism, Footsteps of famous Theologians, World Peace & Harmony, Global Capitalism, Network Marketing, Cybertheology, Population & Demographics, Epigraphic Studies, Contextualized Education, and many others. We welcome a Mss. on any topic/s mentioned, whether they are original works, scholarly monographs, collections of conference papers, revised dissertations, or translations of historical documents. Through the Series we, the Publishers, are striving to put forward published works that may help Institutions, Academic Bodies, Researchers, Scholars and the World at large in furthering their respective knowledge and understanding on the concerned subject. We welcome your comments on our efforts and further suggestions on how we can foster the upcoming thought provoking theologically grounded books.

Christian Heritage Rediscovered - 80

Christianity and Health & Educational Development in South Travancore

The Work of the London Missionary Society from 1890 - 1947

M. Christhudhas

Christian World Imprints

First Published in 2019 by

Christian World Imprints
Christian Publishing & Books from India
H-12 Bali Nagar, **New Delhi-110015**
info@christianworldimprints.com
www.ChristianWorldImprints.com
Phone: +91 11 25465925

ISBN: 978-93-5148-356-4 (HB)
ISBN: 978-93-5148-357-1 (PB)

Printed in India.

Contents

Foreword

I appreciate Rev. Dr M. Christhudhas for his commitment to study and research from a pastoral perspective, in bringing out the book *Christianity and Health & Educational Development in South Travancore :The Work of the London Missionary Society from 1890 - 1947*. The book provides a comprehensive and critical outlook on the health care and education activities of the London Missionary Society (LMS) in the present Kanyakumari District of Tamil Nadu for the students of mission history to understand and interpret the contribution of the missionary movement to the healing and empowerment of communities.

The book provides an inspiring and elaborate reading of the mission history in pre-independent India (1890-1947), following a historical and descriptive methodology. In a seemingly tolerant and peaceful religious context, which was in fact volatile and violent, through the practice of stringent caste system, communities were stigmatized, excluded and dehumanized. The book enumerates how the politically powerless, socially oppressed and religiously excluded and marginalized 'no people' were equipped and empowered through education and came to be recognized as 'God's people'. The book also narrates the story of how missionaries opened opportunities of education to all without discrimination and recognized the right to education as primary for the transformation of communities.

The healing mission of LMS not only provided basic care and healing to those who had no access to health facilities but ensured a right to health to the marginalized, especially to women and children. Healing in fact meant not just treatment to ailments but journeying with and accompanying people in their struggles and problems counselling them, giving them assurance and courage as well as returning their human dignity and honour.

The author helps the reader to travel back in time to understand and to imbibe the vision of transforming gospel to the present education and healing mission of the Church in the light of the historical legacy. The author empowers the present generation to understand how education and healing could bring about transformation through liberation, emancipation, empowerment, reconciliation, healing and harmony in the communities.

While thanking the author for giving me this privilege to write a few lines as foreword to his work, I appreciate the committed efforts of Rev. M. Christhudhas, a senior Presbyter of CSI Kanyakumari diocese who also served as the Treasurer as well as the Secretary of the Pastoral Concerns of the diocese, in bringing his research to fruition in the form of this book. I wish that Rev. Dr M. Christhudhas may be given grace to continue to contribute to the scholarly discourse further through research and study so as to bring joy and benefit of the knowledge and wisdom to many and inspire the Church to be more diligent and faithful in the entrusted ministry, especially in the field of education and healing.

Rev. Dr. D. R. Sadananda
General Secretary, Church of South India

Preface

With delighted heart I present this book entitled *Christianity and Health & Educational Development in South Travancore: The Work of the London Missionary Society from 1890 - 1947*. This book brings out a comprehensive study on the health care and educational activities of London Missionary Society (LMS) in the existing Kanyakumari District of Tamilnadu. It mainly focuses on the work of missionaries in the areas of health care and education during the period of 1890-1947 which have not been amply investigated in the previously presented historical woks. To study on the matter historical and descriptive methodology has been followed. This book covers four chapters that explain elaborately with much analysis on the historical records. The main hypothesis of this research is that London Mission Society contributed largely to the health care and education of the people by establishing various institutions and hospitals throughout the period. This book begins with the study of the Historical context of South Travancore, which observes that, politically, it was a period of British entry in the rule of South Travancore. The society was under caste stigma and it was expressed in the form of various inhuman practices. Religious context was tolerant and peaceful. Further the book narrates the work of the London Missionary Society in South Travancore, who worked among the people who were politically powerless, socially oppressed and religiously segregated. Missionaries worked against the oppressive social practices by implementing developmental programmes for the upliftment of those people. In the next level the book analyses the Health Care Mission in South Travancore. In the context of less medical facilities the missionaries started clinics, dispensaries, hospitals and leprosy homes to meet the medical needs of the people, especially, the poor. This helped the native people to protect their life from the untouchable diseases such as leprosy and cancer and to save the life of women and children during the time of child birth. Finally, the book deals with the Educational mission in South Travancore, which provided higher education to all sections of people, especially, the low caste people. In short, LMS mission contributed a lot to the health care and educational development of South Travancore during the period of 1890-1947.

I hope this book will be useful guide to those who undertake missionary work and organize Christian mission in the grass root level. I hope it will also be beneficial to the academicians of missiology to draw inspiration from the mission body, like, London Missionary Society.

The Rev. Dr. M. Christhudhas
Presbyter & Corporate Manager of Schools
Church of South India, Kanyakumari Diocese
Tamil Nadu, South India

Acknowledgment

I am grateful to God, the Almighty for being with me all through this work and with whose grace I could complete this work successfully.

I am thankful to my Diocese for mending me in my ministerial journey and enabling me to bring out this book.

My deep sense of gratitude goes to my mentor the Rev. Dr. Andreas Gross, who inspired and gave me a desire and passion towards history of Christianity and with whose valuable guidance and effort this work became a great success.

With great honour I extend my heartfelt thanks to the Rev. Dr. Rathnakara Sadananda, the General Secretary of Church of South India for writing the *Foreword* for this book.

I am grateful to the Rev. K. James Cecil Victor, the Director of the Department of Pastoral Concerns, Church of South India Synod and the Rev. Dr. A. Rayappan Isaac, Head of Department & Senior Lecturer, Church History, Pacific Theological College, Suva, Fiji for writing few words about the book.

I offer my gratitude to the Rev. Dr. Gnana Robinson for his help towards my M.Th. studies and to my friends, Rev. S. Christopher Yesumony, Rev. M. Albert Sutha Gnanadhas, Rev. S. Jeyalal, Rev. A. Bright Solomon, Rev. N. Vibin John, Rev. S. Arul Jeba Singh, Rev. C. Gildon Dhayananth, Rev. T. P. Salim Thanka Kumar, Rev. Ramesh D. Dhas, Rev. J. Prakash Nayagam, Rev. O. Densingh, Dr. Viju Wilson and Mr. M.R. Milton Mark for their encouragement and support in completing this work successfully.

I am indebted to my parents Mr. P. Muthuswamy (Late) and Mrs. S. Rethinabai for bringing me up and moulding me for God's ministry. I am also thankful to my sister, Mrs. M. Nirmala Kumari Thankamony and my brother, Mr. M. Christopher Babu for their enduring encouragements.

I am obliged to my life partner, Mrs. T. Sheela, for her inestimable support and patient for being with me through my life journey, especially, in doing this work and to my children C.S. Bussard and C.S. Bestlin for cheering me up with their love and affection even during this work.

At this moment, I remember my ever loving gift of God, C.S. Best, my son who lives in memory. I, whole heartedly, dedicate this book to him and for his love.

Author

Introduction

A number of studies have been done on the work and contribution of London Missionary Society (LMS), the pioneer Protestant Missionary Society from England to South Travancore. Since many of them do not highlight the health care and education activities of missionary work, particularly in the period of 1890-1947, a comprehensive study is needed. The modern missionary movement was initiated in the late 18th century in England when the Protestant churches began to think about the missionary work. The missionary zeal among the people gave birth to a number of missionary societies such as Baptist Missionary Society (1792), London Missionary Society (1795), The British and Foreign Bible Society (1805), The American Board of Commissioners for Foreign Mission (1810), Wesleyan Methodist Missionary Society (1813), Basel Evangelical Mission (1815), and the Committee for Foreign Missions of the General Assembly of the Church of Scotland (1824). The London Missionary Society (LMS) was established by a group of friends-John Ryland, H. O.Wills, John Itey, Robert Stephen and David Bogue on 21st Sept 1795 with a plan and constitution. This attempt was a response to the letter from William Carey regarding the need for missionaries in India. The aim of this Missionary Society was to spread the knowledge of Christ among the non-Christians. Based on the society's aims and principles, it started to send missionaries to different parts of the world.

In the year 1804, LMS sent six missionaries to start mission work in South India and Ceylon. One among them was the Lutheran

Missionary William Topias Ringeltaube from Germany (1770-1816). He came to India in 1804 and was welcomed by the Danish Halle Missionaries in Tranquebar. He was under the guidance of Rev. John Casper Kohlhoff, in Tranquebar till the end of the year 1805, learning Tamil and Indian philosophy. Ringeltaube reached South Travancore on 25th April 1806 and went to Cochin to pay his respect to British Resident Colonel Macaulay and returned to Mylaudy on 1st March 1807 with a well planned programme of mission work with 'Ten-point action plan.' The plan for the mission in South Travancore was based on the invitation he got from a Tamil convert Maharasan Vedamanikam. The LMS was the first Protestant Mission to establish mission stations in South Travancore. The beginning of the work of the LMS was connected with the conversion of a man from south Travancore by name Maharasan Vedamanikam. The LMS started its work in a particular socio-economic-religious-political context of South Travancore. In the early 19th century slavery and bondage prevailed in South Travancore. Economically, religiously and politically high class people enjoyed all the privileges. In this context, missionaries of LMS started its mission by responding to the issues of people.

People of the region were suffering from different kinds of epidemics and medical facilities were not accessible to all. They suffered from various contagious diseases and epidemics which were regular and seasonal. The scourges like Cholera, Small Pox, and Malaria consumed hundreds of human lives and majority who died of this scourges belonged to the unprivileged sections of society. In this context, the health care work was started by the Protestant Missionary Archibald Ramsey in 1838 at Nagercoil. The following Protestant Medical Missionaries continued the health care work from the year 1890 to 1947, namely, Sargood Fry (1886-1892), Mac Donnel (Nurse) 1890-1906, Arther Fells (1893-1901). William Charles Bentall (1902-1907), James Davidson (1905-1913), S. H. Pugh (1913-1926), G. A. P. Thomas (1913-1916) and T. Howard Samerwell (1924-1949). These missionaries made an earnest attempt at the expansion of the mission particularly starting the health care units in the mostly needed places like Shanthapuram, Nagercoil, Kottaram, Thittuvilai, Marthandam, Kulashekaram and

Neyyoor. They have started department of nursing at Neyyoor for imparting health care education. The important one among them was the Charles Peace Memorial Leprosy Hospital Neyyoor on 11th August 1892.

In a context where education was the monopoly of high-caste people, the LMS missionaries took initiatives to open educational benefits to low-caste people and women. The first English School started in 1809 at Mylaudy and was established by Ringeltaube. This was indeed the first English School from Mylaudy. It was transferred to Nagercoil and it was known as 'Seminary'. Gradually, the Protestant Missionaries understood that only education could change the society. So they started schools from Koodenkulam to Thengapattanam of South Travancore. The school, namely 'Bazaar School' was started in 1820 at Nagercoil bazaar to eradicate the prejudices of the caste system which prevailed in the society. The first girls' school was started with the help of the missionary wives namely Mrs. Mead, Mrs. Mault, Mrs. Miller and Mrs. Thompson in 1820 at Nagercoil. Slaves and orphans were admitted in these schools. On 26th October 1896, the foundation stone was laid for the first college in South Travancore, known as Scott Christian College. The following missionaries contributed much for higher education between the year 1890-1947, namely James Duthie (1860-1908) and Robert Sinclair (1908-1939).

The LMS missionaries arrived to South Travancore as Church planters, women emancipationalists, educationists, doctors and nurses to liberate the people from their social oppressive structures. They planted churches, established schools; hospital and health care units. The health care and educational work of the Protestant Missionaries helped the people to save their lives from the epidemics and social oppression. But the Protestant Missionaries' contributions to the health care and education, especially during 1890 to 1947, were not researched comprehensively in the historical works available on LMS in South Travancore of the present Kanyakumari district of Tamil Nadu.

This research is an attempt to record comprehensively the contributions of the Protestant Missionaries to health care and education in South Travancore of 1890-1947, particularly in the present Kanyakumari District of Tamilnadu. Geographically, South Travancore stretches between Quilon in Kerala and Kanyakumari in Tamilnadu. For mission purpose the LMS divided South Travancore into six mission districts, namely, Quilon, Attingal, Trivandrum, and Parasalla in Kerala, Neyyoor and Nagercoil in Tamilnadu. The present research is focused only on two mission districts Neyyoor and Nagercoil which extends to four revenue taluks of present Kanyakumari district. Since the LMS started to concentrate more on education and health care from 1890 onwards, and continued till the formation of CSI in 1947, the study focuses on the contributions of LMS to health care and education in South Travancore during the period of 1890 to 1947.

The methodology of this research is historical and descriptive. The researcher will examine and evaluate the primary documents such as annual reports, letters, minutes and the secondary sources which have come out in the form of books, articles, journals, unpublished thesis in Tamil and English. Many studies have been made on the contributions of LMS, but the researcher has not found any research on health care and education activities of LMS, especially during the period 1890-1947.

The research has four chapters. The first chapter deals with the historical context of South Travancore. It covers the socio-political-religious situation of South Travancore at the arrival of LMS missionaries. The second chapter concentrates on the London missionary society in South Travancore. It briefly explains the origin and the various activities of missionaries. The third chapter focuses on the health care of LMS in South Travancore. It highlights the major contributions of LMS in the development of health care. The fourth chapter narrates the educational mission of LMS in South Travancore. It describes the contributions of LMS in the field of education.

Chapter 1

The Historical Context of South Travancore

Introduction

South Travancore, a princely state located in the extreme south of peninsular India, had customs and traditions. Being dominated by the high caste Brahmins, many disabilities prevailed in the society due to caste hierarchy and oppression. It was because of the awakening of the Protestant missionaries of the London Missionary Society,[1] people started to agitate against the social evils and human rights violations. The primary object of the missionary society was to spread the gospel in a society in which where inequality, injustice and oppression reigned supreme. When the missionaries arrived in India in 1806, the present Kanyakumari District was part of Travancore state. Since Kanyakumari lays in the extreme south of Travancore State, it was referred as South Travancore province. During the arrival of missionaries in South Travancore, the society was literally divided on the basis of caste.

The low caste people were treated as slaves by the land lords. The rulers were also under the impression that it was their sacred

1 Hereafter cited as LMS.

duty or '*Dharma*' to maintain the existing inequality among the people. Ordinary men and women were under the stigma of social customs and religious rituals. In such a situation the missionaries worked to liberate those oppressed human beings from the clutches of dehumanizing social, religious, economic and political systems. Due to the committed missionary activity and the gradual rise of a native Christian community, this region has attracted a fair degree of scholarly attention. In order to bring out the significance of the work of LMS missionaries in the areas of health care and education, a background study of this particular period is needed. Hence, in this chapter is a description of the geographical, socio-religious, economic and political background of South Travancore.

1. Geographical Sketch of South Travancore

Geographically the original designation of Travancore was '*Chera*' or as we find it and spelt by some authors '*Sera.*'[2] The place Kanyakumari, once known as the Granary of Travancore lies at the South-Western part of Indian Peninsula. It was a part of Travancore for a long time and then merged with Tamil Nadu in 1956 under the State Linguistic Reorganization Act.[3] Travancore has been rightly called the Garden of India for it is a green and fertile land.[4] Travancore is the abbreviated English form of '*Tiru-vithankodu*', once the capital of the kingdom and the residence of the Royal court, but now a petty village that lay 30 miles to the South East of Trivandram. Tirruvithankodu is said to be a correction of '*Sri-Vazhu- Kodu*', i.e., a place where the Goddess, of Prosperity dwells. It was also believed that Thiruvithancode is the later form of Srivalumkadu which is said to be the place of many

2 P. Shanoony Menon, *A History of Travancore from the Earlier Times*, Madras: Higginbotham and Co, 1887, 1.

3 S. C. Bhatt, '*Kanyakumari*': *The Encyclopedic District Gazetteers of India, Vol. 2*, New Delhi: Gyan Publishing House, 1998, 1079.

4 John A Jacob, *A History of the London Missionary Society in South Travancore, 1806-1959*, Nagercoil: The Diocesan Press, 1990, 1.

goddesses.[5] Travancore was one of the loveliest parts of India, of which it may truly be said, "Here is God's plenty."[6]

South Travancore is also known by the name of '*Venad*', '*Vanchi-Desam*' and '*Tiru-Adi-Desam*'. Venad is a correction of '*Vanavanad*' (the land of the celestials). Vanchi-Desam means either the land of Treasure or the land of bamboos. '*Tiru-Adi-Desam*' is probably derived from "*tiru-Adikal*' means 'holy feet' or 'the royal feet. Malankarai is another name for Travancore used exclusively by the Syrian Christians and the Syrian Christians' Metropolitan is still called as "The *Malankarai Metran*"[7] *Travancore is known to be Karma-Bhumi* (land of action), *Gnana-Bhumi* (Land of knowledge), and *Punnya-Bhumi* (land of charity). In 1956, when the Indian States were reorganized, the four Taluks of Travancore; Vilavancode, Kalkulam, Thovala and Agusteeswaram were united to form the present Kanyakumari District and were integrated with the state of Madras which later became Tamil Nadu State. The rest of the Travancore became part of Kerala State. The land had early trade relations with other neighboring countries. The land was rich in its natural fertility and had a lot of valuable goods. This region consisted of a long and narrow strip of land, 174 miles in length with a medium breadth inland of 40 miles.[8] South Travancore has many beautiful places, besides Cap-Comorin or Kanyakumari. The district has been named after the goddess Kanyakumari Amman who is the popular deity of the area. Kanyakumari consist with four taluks namely Vilavancode, Kalkulam, Thovala and Agusteeswaram. The boundaries of Kanyakumari are Tirunelveli in the North and North-

---

5 S. S. Hector, *Thiruchabbai Varalaru (Tamil) Vol. I*, Nagercoil: Kanyakumari Diocese, 1988, 5.

6 Joy Gnanadason, *A Forgotten History: The Story of the Missionary Movement and the Liberation People in South Travancore*, Madras: Gurukul Lutheran Theological College and Research Institute, 1994, 15.

7 V. Nagam Aiya, *The Travancore State Manual,* Vol.III, New Delhi: Asian Educational Services, 1989, 2 & 3.

8 Dick Kooiman, *Conversion and Social Equality in India*, New Delhi: Manohar Publishers, 1989, 13.

East, Kerala State in the North-West and Arabian Sea and Indian Ocean on the West and South. It has its head quarters at Nagercoil.[9]

2. The Political Structure of South Travancore

2.1. Before 1800 A.D

India has been known to the world for its diverse cultures and civilization. Indus Valley Civilization, the oldest Indian civilization, dates back to over 5000 years. Because of its vast richness and resources, India had been the target of many invaders. Travancore was one of the fifty six kingdoms into which India seem to have been divided in ancient times, and under this name it holds a high place in Puranic literature, besides being mentioned in the two great Indian epics, the Ramayana and the Mahabaratha.[10] In the early period women were given all privileges and untouchability was not in practice.[11]

In the 4th century B. C. various invaders like the Turks, the Muslim, and the Moguls invaded India. Even before Vasco da Gama, the Portuguese sailor – adventurer who had made his momentous landing in Calicut, four major kingdoms had emerged on the political landscape of Kerala: Venad, Cochin, Calicut and Kolathunadu. Padmanabhapuram in Kalkulam Taluk (now in Tamilnadu) was a capital of Venad and it extended from Kanyakumari to Edava.[12] Venad was expanded largely and became a powerful military state.[13]

These kingdoms were attacked by several other neighboring kings. South Travancore faced this attack from the kings of Venad, Mysore and Madurai. The powerful kings used the military forces to extent their territory. In 825 the king Udaya Marthanda-Varma,

---

9 S. C. Bhatt , *The Encyclopedic District Gazetteers of India*, 1079.

10 I. H. Hacker, *A Hundred Years in Travancore, A Centenary Memorial Volume of the Work of the London Missionary Society, South India*, London: H. R. Allenson Limited, 1908, 11.

11 A. Sreedhara Menon, *A Survey of Kerala History*, New Delhi, 1980, 79.

12 V. Jamal Mohammed, "Kerala", in *Dravidian Encyclopedia,* edited by Subramanian, Vol. II, Thiruvananthapuram: The International School of Dravidian Linguistic, 1993, 381.

13 T. K. Velu Pillai, *The Travancore State Manual, Vol. III,* Trivandrum: 1940, 104.

ruled in Venad, attacked and encroached a part of Travancore and formed Quilon.[14] The Travancore kingdom was ruled by king Karunandadakkan from the year 857 to 885. In his period he bought property from '*Munchari Sabha*' and constructed a Vishnu temple and also named the place as '*Parthivasekharapuram*'.[15] In the 11th century the region fell under the Chola Empire. Ravi Varma was another important king ruled Venad from the year 1299 to 1314. Vasco da Gama came in the year 1498 to Kallicode of Arabian sea side. After his arrival Portuguese and British began to use Travancore both for trade and residential purpose (Before used only for trade).[16]

At the end of the 15th century western countries took interest in India. Thus the Portuguese, the Dutch, and the French came in quick succession apparently with the purpose of trade. The Hindu kings of the Vijaya Nagar Empire held it briefly in the 16th century and later it was under the control of Muslim rule. In 1684, Attingal Rani gave the place called Anchu Thenggu to East India Company for residential use.[17] In the middle of the 18th century, the region was unified and became the independent state of Travancore, allied with the British in their wars in Southern India. Later, Travancore came under the rule of Perumals. After the death of the last Perumal, the country was divided into three parts known as *Thekkae mukham* (region facing South), *Vadekkae mukham* (region facing North) and *Padignarary mukham* (region facing west).[18]

The modern history of Travancore begins with Marthanda Varma, (1729-1758),[19] the father of modern Travancore. He maintained friendly relationship with the English East India

---

14 G. Christhudhas, *Paathachuvadukal*, CMS Printing Press, Palayamkottai, 2005, 6.

15 A. Sreedhara Menon, *A Survey of Kerala History*, 79.

16 G. Christhudhas, *Paathachuvadukal*, 7.

17 G. Christhudhas, *Paathachuvadukal*, 7.

18 Samuel Zechariah, *A Summary of the History of the Church in South Travancore, Vol.1*, (Tamil), Nagercoil: 1897, 5.

19 Marthanda Varma was a king ruling in Travancore. During the second half of the 18th century, the sultans of Mysore became very powerful in South India. In 1766, Hyder Alikhan made a conquest in the Northern parts of Kerala. He got victory over Calicut and made Cochin a tributary but Travancore was spared.

Company.[20] He imposed heavy taxes over the low caste people and the newly implemented 'head *tax*' in the year 1754 on Nadar community remaines unforgettable. He also offered Travancore to '*Lord Padmanaba*'[21] on 3rd January 1758 and paved the way for Brahmin and Nair domination in South Travancore. On 31st July 1741 he prevented the Dutch army and not to encroach the places belong to South Travancore from Colachel to Thenkapattanam. And also in the war he defeated the Dutch army on 10th August 1741. He dedicated himself and the land to the Lord Padmanaba on 3rd January 1750. After this victory he called himself as 'Padmanabadhasa' (servant of Lord Badmanabha). From this period the kings of Travancore were considered to be the representatives of Sri Padmanabha.[22] In Marthanda Varma's time Travancore was divided into four main stations namely, Padmanabhapuram, Trivandram, Quilon, and Certhallai.[23]

Rama Varma ruled Travancore from the year 1758 to 1798. During the second half of the 18th century, the Sultans of Mysore became very powerful in south India. In 1766, Hyder Ali made a conquest in the northern parts of Kerala. He conquered Calicut and made Cochin a tributary and kept the Travancore under his control and out of danger.[24] After his death in 1782, his son Tippu Sultan succeeded him.[25] Sultan king was not good with the people of Travancore because they were not obedience to the implementations of tax and other suppressing attitudes of the king. The king started to disturb the people in many unwanted ways. Therefore in 1795, to save Travancore from the hand of Sultans King Ravi Varma was friendly with the East India Company. The British sent military to

---

After his death in 1782, his son Tippu Sultan succeeded him (T. K. Velu Pillai, *The Travancore State Manual,* Vol. II, 104).

20 J. W. Gladstone, *Protestant Christianity and People's Movements in Kerala, 1850-1936,* Trivandrum: The Seminary Publications, KUTC, 1984, 50.

21 Padmanabha was a deity, worshiped by the people of Travancore.

22 V. Nagam Aiya, *The Travancore State Manual, Vol. 1,* 362.

23 T. K. Velu Pillai, *Travancore State Manual, Vol. 1,* 16.

24 T. K. Velu Pillai, *Travancore State Manual, Vol. I,* Trivandrum: 1940, 382.

25 P. Shungoonny Menon, *A History of Travancore from the Earlier Times,* 206.

Travancore for protection. This paved the way for having a British Resident in Travancore. Tippu Sultan was not friendly with the East India Company and the war between both continued, finally Tippu Sultan was killed by the English at Seringapattanam in 1799.[26] One of the divided stations in the time of Marthanda Varma, Padmanabhapuram came under South Travancore region where the Protestant Missionaries started their mission work in the early 19th century.

2.2. From 1800 to 1850 A.D

At the end of 18th century, Travancore came under the supremacy of the British.[27] According to the regulations of the treaty relationship with the Danish East India Company in 1800, Travancore received the first British Resident, Col. Colin Macaulay.[28] Velu Thambi, then the Dewan rushed to the Resident for protection because he faced opposition from the Muslim petty kings.[29] He was a man of extraordinary ability and talents. He had strong passions and quick sensibility and was amazingly bold and daring.[30] After 1805, the relationship between the Dewan and the Resident became bitter due to the imposed heavy taxes and also the political and commercial interests of the Resident.[31] Later the Dewans of Cochin and Travancore joined and attacked the Resident on 28th December 1805, but the Resident escaped.[32] Dewan Velu Thambi was killed on 7th November 1810 and the British took full control after his death.[33]

In 1811, Col. Munro was asked to accept the Office of Dewan. He allowed the Protestant missionary enterprise in Travancore.[34] The Resident was in power and the petty rulers were assigned to rule

26 G. Christhudhas, *Paathachuvadukal, 8.*

27 J.W. Gladstone, *Protestant Christianity and People's Movements in Kerala,* 52.

28 R. N. Yesudas, *British Policy in Travancore,* Trivandrum: N.p., 1977, 14.

29 J. W. Gladstone, *Protestant Christianity and People's Movements in Kerala*, 53.

30 P. Shanoony Menon, *A History of Travancore from the Earlier Times*, 300.

31 J. W. Gladstone, *Protestant Christianity and People's Movements in Kerala,* 52.

32 P. Shanoony Menon, *A History of Travancore from the Earlier Times,* 39.

33 P. Shanoony Menon, *A History of Travancore from the Earlier Times,* 359.

34 J. W. Gladstone, *Protestant Christianity and People's Movements in Kerala*, 55.

Travancore and those rulers were very much submissive to the British power. From the year 1810 to 1815 Howri Leshmibai, from 1815 to 1829 Howri Parvathi Bai, and from 1829 to 1847 Suvathi Tirunal Rama Varma ruled as a petty kings of South Travancore with the help and guidance of British Resident.[35] In the beginning, the Resident was very supportive of the high castes. It is evident in the adoption of Travancore state emblem which had two elephants with raised trunks and a conch; and a Sanskrit motto meaning "Charity our Household Divinity," because those elements placed in the emblem were considered as the status symbols of the high castes.[36]

2.3. From 1850 to 1947 A.D

By 1850 A. D. the British took full possession of India and except few areas to the French (Pondicherry, Karaikal and Mahle), to the Portuguese (Goa, Daman, and Diu) and to the Dutch, (Tarangambadi and nearby areas).[37] From the year 1847 to 1860 Uttram Thirunal, 1860 to 1880 Ayilliam Thriunal, 1880 to 1885 Vizagam Thriunal, 1885 to 1924 Moolam Thirunal Rama Varma were assigned to rule Travancore by the British Resident. The policy of the English East India Company before 1900 was guided by the commercial interests because Travancore had a long coast and favorable items of trade. The British Policy in India allowed the existence of individual kingdoms as long as they were able and willing to continue under the British.[38]

The British were more powerful in Travancore and people of Travancore were more dependable on them for their own developments and daily needs. The assigned rulers were fully controlled by the British. The king Moolam Thirunal Rama Varma (1885 to 1924) was the prime mover to bring Democratic Rule in Travancore state. He formed people Court and Legislate Assembly. Sedhu Leshmibai ruled from 1924 to 1931 and Bala Varma from

35 G. Christhudhas, *Paathachuvadukal*, 9.

36 Joy Gnanadason, *A Forgotten History*, 13.

37 E. L. Clement, A Paper presented on Kanyakumari Diocese' Contribution to Nation Building, in an International Seminar on "Bearing Witness to the God made known in Christ in India Today" at Peace Trust Kanyakumari on 23. 08. 2006, 1.

38 G. Christhudhas, *Paathachuvadukal*, 9.

1931 to 1947 after this period the kingship was vanished from Travancore. Missionary work made the people to think of having freedom from the oppressive structures. People of this part enriched with human awareness and spirit of nationalism. India was freed from the hand of the British and got independence on 15th August 1947. In the beginning of the 20th century, the political situation became favorable to the work of the Protestant Missionaries in South Travancore.[39]

3. The Social Context and Customs

3.1. Caste System

During the early years of Travancore state, people shared a common cultural heritage. People of different communities lived together in harmony, following their different vocations. They had no stigma of caste differences and lived in peace with one another. But by the arrival of Brahmins into Travancore around the 10th century, the whole scenario changed. In the 12th century, the caste system was firmly established in Travancore.[40] It is believed that the Society was subjected to casteism by the invasion of Aryans.[41] According to the Aryan ideal society, there are four major distinctions in the caste system namely *Brahmanas, Vaishayas, Kshatriyas and Shudras.*[42] V. Nagam Aiya, in his book writes about twenty six names of different castes in Travancore.[43] In Travancore the higher castes were the Brahmins, the Nambudiris and the Nairs. The Lower Castes were

39 J.W. Gladstone, *Protestant Christianity and People's Movements in Kerala,* 56.

40 Joy Gnanadason, *A Forgotten History,* 19.

41 M. K. Sharma, *Dalit Voice, Nair Women of Kerala,* Vol. 7, Bangalore: Oct 16-31, No. 23, 2005, Quoted by Bhanu Samuel in his B.D. Thesis, *Vedamanikam*, Gurukul Lutheran Theological College and Research Institute, Chennai, 1997, 7.

42 M.K. Sharma, *Dalit Voice, Nair Women of Kerala*, Vol. 7, 14.

43 Twenty six caste names: Brahmins, Arya Pattars, Pattattiyars, The Malavala Kshatriyas, Nambidis, Muttan, Ilayatu, Kodi pattars, Aris, Ambalavasis, Samantas, Nayars, Marans, Krishmanyagakkars, Nanjanad Vellalars, Pattaryars, Dasis, Konkani, Brahmins, Kudumi Chettis, Kammalrs, Shanars, Izhavas, Kuravars, Pariahs, Pulayas, Hill Tribes (V. Nagam Aiya, *The Travancore State Manual, Asian Educational Services, Vol. 11*, New Delhi: 1989, 245-420).

the Nadar and Ezhavas. The slave castes were the Sambavars, the Pariahs and the Pulayas. The Brahmins, the Kshatriyas, the Vaisyahs and the Shudras considered others as having no caste.[44] The society in the beginning of 19th century was based mainly on the institution of caste. Lower castes were permitted to approach the higher ones only up to a prescribed number of steps and the greater the ritual distance, the greater the spatial separation. Nowhere in India was the caste system as rigid as in Travancore.[45] The vast majority of the depressed poor like the Ezhavas, Nadars, Parayas, etc., were socially marginalized and ritually discriminated.[46]

'Brahmins'[47] were the dominant section in the land of South Travancore, who considered themselves as superior and subjected all the other native people by holding higher Government positions and power.[48] In Travancore the vast majority of the people were virtually the slaves of dominant castes like Brahmins. The term Brahmin is derived from *Brahma,* the creator from whose mouth the Brahmins are said to have sprung and hence their caste name.[49] They had extraordinary control over the Kings and influenced the state politics. Thus gradually, it came to be accepted that things related to royalty would become legal only if the Brahmins performed all the ceremonies connected with the enthronement. The kings of the Travancore also regarded that their sacred duty is to please the Brahmins and to rule the country in accordance with the advice of

44 Bishop G. Christdas, *Paachuvadukal, History of Church of South India in Kanyakumari Diocese* (Tamil), Palayamkottai: CMS Printing Press, 2005, 9.

45 J. W. Gladstone, 19th Century Mass Movement In South Travancore- A Result of Social Liberation, *Indian Church History Review*, Vol. X / 1, June 1976, The Wesley Press, Mysore, 56.

46 V. Sathianesan, *Reconversion Impulse in Travancore*, Indian Church History Review, Vol. XXV1/ 1, June 1992, Church History Association, Banglore, 5.

47 Brahmins are considered as the actual lord of the soil. Brahmin comes from the Sanskrit word "Brahmana" means a person who possesses the supreme Sacred Knowledge – Vedic Knowledge. It denotes the highest ranking Varna or Caste in the Hindu Social hierarchy (I.H. Hacker, *A Hundred Years in Travancore* 14).

48 S.S. Hector, *History of the Church, Kankakumari Diocese 1806 to 1907.* (Tamil), *Vol. 1, Dioceson Press, Nagercoil,* 8.

49 V. Jamal Mohammed, Edited by V.I. Subramanian, "Kerala", in *Dravidian Encyclopedia,* 120.

Brahmin scholars and counsels. The kings spent a large sum of money for the support sustenance and the comfort of the Brahmins.[50]

The 'Nambudir's' were another exclusive caste group of Brahmins peculiar to Malabar. They were believed to be the true Aryans in southern India.[51] These people were medical practitioners who traced their medical knowledge from the instructions given by Parasurama, a legendary Conqueror of Kerala.[52] Proud and arrogant, the Nambudiris led very secluded lives and many of them devoted themselves to the performance of religious ceremonies in temples. The unlimited social, economic, political and religious powers enjoyed by them were a barrier to the progress of the people. Travancore society virtually staggered under their domination.[53]

Nairs[54] were the ruling group of the country, dominating in political, economic and military affairs.[55] The Nairs lived in joint families. In the 11th and 12th centuries, the Nairs formed the feudal aristocracy owning most of the land in Travancore. In Travancore, the Nairs with other indigenous castes formed a huge militia that was maintained by the state. In the latter part of the 18th century, Maharajah Rama Varma had a hundred thousand soldiers. Most of them were Nairs who were armed with bows, spears, swords and battle axes.[56] A century and more of peaceful rule has wrought material change in the character of the people. They became engrossed in

---

50 J.W. Gladstone, *Protestant Christianity and People's Movements in Kerala*, 23.

51 V. Nagam Aiya, *The Travancore State Manual*, Vol. 11, 247.

52 Koji Kawashima, *Missionaries and a Hindu State of Travancore, 1858-1936*, Delhi: Oxford University Press, 1998, 141.

53 Joy Gnanadason, *A Forgotten History*, 21.

54 The word 'Nair' derives from the Sanskrit term "Nayaka" meaning "leader". Though these Nairs were subordinate to Brahmins, they dominated over other castes. The people who were ready to serve the Brahmins were formed with a new caste, the Nairs (V. Jamal Mohammed, edited by Subramanian, Kerala", in *Dravidian Encyclopedia* 522. J.W. Gladstone, *Protestant Christianity and People's Movements in Kerala*, 25).

55 Dick Kooiman, *Conversion and Social Equality in India*, 17.

56 V. Nagam Aiya, *The Travancore State Manual*, Vol. 11, 346.

agriculture, Government service or their own affairs and had won themselves the name of powerful citizens.[57]

Nadar's in the 19th century were one of the significant agricultural castes.[58] The hereditary occupation of the Nadars was that of cultivating and climbing the Palmyra tree, the juice of which they boil into a coarse sugar.[59] The Nadars were considered to be "a half-polluting" caste even though they were free from some of the restrictions placed on the still lower castes. They were not allowed to carry umbrellas, to use footwear or carry water-pots on their hips. They could not milk cows or use balances to weigh tobacco and other articles. They could not build houses above one storey nor tile them. Their women could not use fine jewels. Their women were forbidden to wear anything whatever above their waist but had to go about clad in a piece of coarse cloth called "*Mundu*" stretching from waist to knees exposing their breasts.[60] They were industrious and hard working people. They lived socially degraded and economically exploited. The Nadars lived in a state of fear, humiliation and despised until the arrival of the British who played a vital role in the affairs of Travancore in the 19th century.[61] For a long time, Nadars had to suffer many social disabilities and harsh economic oppression. Because of these unfortunate circumstances, missionary sources claim that the Nadars had become 'timid', 'deceitful and ignorant'.[62]

57 Joy Gnanadason, *A Forgotten History*, 22.

58 The Nadar are seen in the state of Tamil Nadu and in the Southern part of Kerala. Earlier they were called as shanars. Nadars of South Travancore were the people migrated from Tirunelvelli District of Tamilnadu. They belong to one of the races that are commonly known as Dravidians and their mother tongue is Tamil. They generally use the term Nadar along with their names. At the arrival of missionaries, they were thickly populated in the places like Eranel, Vilavancode, Agasteeswaram, Kalkulam and Neyyattinkara in the Travancore State. In appearance they are a darkened skinned race with low foreheads, sunken eyes and prominent cheekbones (V. Nagam Aiya, *The Travancore State Manual,* Vol. 11, 392f).

59 J.W. Gladstone, *Protestant Christianity and People's Movements in Kerala,* 27.

60 Joy Gnanadason, *A Forgotten History*, 26.

61 Joy Gnanadason, *A Forgotten History*, 27.

62 Dick Kooiman, *Conversion and Social Equality in India*, 15.

Ezhavas were known by different caste names: in Travancore 'Ezhavas', in Malabar to Calicut as 'Teers'. They were another group of "lower castes" but above "the outcastes".[63] Their cultivation was the coconut palms. They tapped the juice from them and manufactured toddy. Their women were very skilled in the preparation of the coir-fiber and the manufacture of coir-ropes. Some of them were also boatmen and weavers.[64]

Economically, they were backward and socially they suffered the same harassment as the Nadars in the hands of the Government and the "high castes".[65] The internal economy of this caste was regulated by the head man who received their title of *Tantan* or *Ponampan* or *Panikkan* from the Rajas and local chiefs. Latter in Travancore their social head men were known as *Channarmar*, *Mutul Pattukar* and *Perambanmar*.[66] The religion of the Ezhavas was Hinduism, but of the Dravidian type rather than the Aryan. They were more Saivite than Vaishnavite. Rice was their staple food. The first rice-feeding ceremony takes place when the child is six months old.[67] They had to maintain 36 feet distance from the Brahmins, as they were one of the "polluted castes".[68] The education standard of this community was not very high. In fact the upper caste did not tolerate the educational development of this caste, even when it got the possibility during the 19th century.[69] Joint family system was common among Ezhavas, who constituted nearly a third of the entire population of the Travancore state with independent occupations.

'Pulaya' and 'Pariah'[70] were the early inhabitants of Travancore. They were found throughout Travancore. These Pariahs and Pulayas

---

63 J.W. Gladstone, *Protestant Christianity and People's Movements in Kerala*, 31.

64 V. Nagam Aiya, *The Travancore State Manual*, Vol. 11, 401.

65 Joy Gnanadason, *A Forgotten History*, 27.

66 K.P. Padmanabha Menon, *History of Kerala, Vol. 111*, edited by T.K. Krishna Menon, New Delhi: Asian Educational Services, 1993, 432 & 433.

67 K.P. Padmanabha Menon, *History of Kerala, Vol. 111*, 442.

68 J.W. Gladstone, *Protestant Christianity and People's Movements in Kerala*, 32.

69 J.W. Gladstone, *Protestant Christianity and People's Movements in Kerala*, 35.

70 Pulayah and pariah; Both were found in Malabar and also scattered in some parts of Travancore. The term 'Pulaya" is derived from the word 'pula' this means 'ceremonial pollution', taint or defilement. Hence, the term 'Pulaya'

were the major "Slave Castes" in Travancore.[71] They were the back-bone of agriculture in the country where the economy was centered on agriculture to a large extent. The houses they lived were miserable huts formed out of sticks and wood, with walls of reed or mud and thatched with grass or coconut leaf, situated by the side of rice swamps without the possibility of polluting "respectable people'. Their dress and habits were extremely grimy. Slaves could not speak the language of the ordinary people.[72] The women of lower castes were only allowed to wear round their neck the strings of beads and small shells. Gold and Silver ornaments they could not of afford to get and, even if they could, till recently, they would not have been allowed to wear them by the higher castes.[73] The caste system became so strong that it was regarded as the duty of a Nair to punish any Pulaya or Pariah who did not get out of the way of the Brahmin. Krishna Iyer spoke of animistic practices among Pariahs and Pulayas, modified in the direction of orthodox Hinduism.[74]

3.2. Slavery

Slavery[75] in South Travancore became hereditary unlike in other parts of India where it existed. Once born to a slave family, the person remained as slave all through the life. Dharma Bhoomi, the land

---

means 'polluted man'. The word Pariah comes from 'parai' or drum' as the caste furnishes the drummers, especially at funerals. They were dark in complexion, strong, muscular in build and capable of a great deal of work. (V. Nagam Aiya, *The Travancore State Manual, Vol. 11,* 402f).

71 V. Nagam Aiya, *The Travancore State Manual, Vol. 11,* 403.

72 S.S. Hector, *History of the Church, Kankakumari Diocese 1806 to 1907*, 8-9.

73 K.P. Padmanabha Menon, *History of Kerala, Vol. 111*, 484.

74 J.W. Gladstone, *Protestant Christianity and People's Movements in Kerala*, 28.

75 The upper caste prohibited "The lower Caste" people from drawing water from the public wells, from studying in the public schools and from entering into their temples. Slavery was allowed and legalized until 1856 when the Temple Entry Act was proclaimed. The Socio-economic status of the lower and out caste was miserable and they lived for decades under the total subjection of the so-called high castes. Lower Caste was permitted to approach the higher ones only up to a prescribed number of steps (Dick Kooiman, *Conversion and Social Equality in India,* 15).

of Charity had become the land of *Adharma*, the home of slavery.[76] About one-third of the population of South Travancore was made up of untouchable communities.[77] Demonism in one shape or the other may be said to rule the Nadars with undisputed authority. In fact the low castes and slave castes were under slavery. These people were not able to raise their voice against this inhuman system. One example for this practice was the low caste Shanar/Nadar women of South Travancore who were not permitted by the upper castes to wear any clothes above the waist.[78] In 1822, Christian women of Kalkulam in South Travancore were openly insulted in public places for wearing upper cloth.[79] The Hindu Shanar women were also not allowed by the high caste Hindus to wear upper cloth.[80] The main reason behind this evil practice was the social structure based on the caste system. Due to slavery in South Travancore, the low caste people were in a state of total subjugation to the minority of the upper caste people in their socio-religious, economic and political life.[81]

3.3. Child Marriage

One of the social evils that enslaved women was the practice of child marriage. The rich and the upper caste people enjoyed this prevailing system. Though the so-called low caste people were not subjected to this evil practice, they were disturbed much by its stigma. In the beginning of 19th century, girls were married off before attaining puberty. Visscher, a Dutch Christian Missionary who was working at Cochin from 1717-1723 pointed out that Brahmins used to give

---

76 Joy Gnanadason, *A Forgotten History*, 28.

77 Dick Kooiman, *Conversion and Social Equality in India,* 16.

78 D. Arthur Jeyakumar, *History of Christianity in India- Selected Themes*, (Madurai: Tamilnadu Theological Seminary, 2000), 59 & 60.

79 Dr. M. Jezer Jebanesan, paper presentation on Mission: *As a Movement of Liberation of the oppressed in South Travancore, in an International Seminar on "Bearing Witness to the God made known in Christ in India Today"* at Peace Trust Kanyakumari on 23. 08. 2006, p. 7.

80 M.K. Kuriakose, *History of Christianity in India; Source Material,* 184-191.

81 K.M. Mathew, *Manorama Year Book, "History of Kerala, 27th year of Publication, Malayala Manorama,* Title, *'Religious Life of the Travancore'* Kottayam- Kerala: 1992, 125.

their daughters in marriage at the age of 8 or 9 years. If they passed their 20th year unmarried they would lose their caste, and were not allowed to marry.[82] Child marriage also existed among the Syrian Christians.[83]

3.4. Devadasi System

Devadasies were the dancing girls in the temple. They were regarded as the maid servants of God. But in reality the Devadasies were temple prostitutes.[84] According to statistics there were 12,000 temple women in South India in 1906. This was a system, which degraded the status of women in the society.[85] The '*pula pedi*'[86] was a social

---

82 R.J. Hepzy Joy, *History and Development of Education of Women in Kerala*, Trivandrum: KUTS, Seminary Publication, 1995, 37.

83 Child marriage was practiced among the Christians; there was a common notion that if there is a girl under or about the age of 14, she is eligible for marriage. Among Jacobites, boys were married at age of 10 or 12 and the girls between 6 or 7. In child marriages, the girl had to live with the groom and had to work hard in the house. One survey shows that in the year 1891 in South Travancore there were child wives- 26 at the age between 0-4, 1129 at 5-9, and 559 at 10-14. (A.H. Day, Dawan *in Travancore*, Kottayam: C.M. Press, 1860, 58).

84 P.N. Kunjan Pillai, *Studies in Kerala History*, Kottayam: National Book Stall, 1970, 282.

85 R.J. Hepzy Joy, *History and Development of Education of Women in Kerala*, 41.

86 It was a social custom or evil that prevailed in South Travancore. The custom of Pula Pedi was directed against the high caste women. According to this practice, during the month of February and March, if a Pulaya man met Nair women without being accompanied by a man she would be polluted. The basic assumption is that the Pulaya man might seize Nair woman if she is alone and that would cause the loss of her caste connections with her relatives because Pulaya man was considered as polluted. In order to avoid such a disgrace, the high caste people observe Pula pedi. The custom of Pula Pedi literally disturbed the normal life of the people. Though this practice was abolished by Unni Kerala Varma, ruler of Venad of Travancore, the system continued as an evil even in the beginning of the 19th century. The high caste Hindu people of South Travancore considered these evil systems as religiously sanctioned one and used them to control the so-called low caste men and women of different caste communities. The people of this region suffered much due to this prevailed evil structure of the society (K.P. Padmanabha Menon, *History of*

custom or evil that prevailed in South Travancore. The custom of Pula Pedi was against the low caste women.[87]

4. Religious Context

4.1. Hinduism

India is the sacred country of Hindus, having been reclaimed from the sea, according to a mythic legend, for the sole use of the Brahmins.[88] Travancore was also known as a purely Hindu State. Hinduism as the religion of the state is contemporary with the colonization of the country by the Brahmin sage.[89] "The higher caste" people had organized worship with permanent temples, priesthood, sacrifice, etc., where as these were absent for "lower castes".[90] Along with Hinduism there were also the minor religions such as Islam, Buddhism, Judaism, Christianity and Jainism.

Hinduism[91] was the dominant religion of the people in South Travancore.[92] The London Missionary Society of South Travancore, Samuel Mateer, in his book describes the nature of Hindus and their temple worship.[93] In South Travancore the most famous

---

Kerala, Vol 11, Ernakulam: Cochin Govt Press, 1929, 274. R.J. Hepzy Joy, *History and Development of Education of Women in Kerala* 42).

87 K.P. Padmanabha Menon, *History of Kerala, Vol 11*, Ernakulam: Cochin Govt Press, 1929, 274.

88 I.H. Hacker, *A Hundred Years in Travancore*, 11.

89 Joy Gnanadason, *A Forgotten History*, 12.

90 V. Nagam Aiya, *The Travancore State Manual, Vol. 11*, 37.

91 The one Supreme Being is worshipped in three aspects in Hinduism as Brahma, Vishnu and Siva, representing respectively the three-fold functions of creation, preservation and destruction. Brahma has no temple anywhere in Travancore that is set apart for his exclusive worship. However, the concept of Triumoorti did not have perennial value since the Vaishnavas and Saivas ascribed the absolute supremacy to Vishnu and Shiva respectively (John A Jacob, *A History of the London Missionary Society in South Travancore, 1806-1959*, 4).

92 Dick Koomian, *Conversion and Social Equality in India*, 15.

93 "Temples were exclusively for the worship of the *Brahmins*. The lower classes had their own temples and deities. They did not dare to touch even the outer walls of the *Brahmin* temples. They could make offerings to the temple only from a distance" (Samuel Mateer, *Native Life in Travancore*, London: London Mission Press, 1883, 333).

Vaishnavite temple of great repute is situated at Thiruvattar, north east of Marthandam, half way between Cape Comorin and Thiruvananthapuram. The most famous Saiva temple in this area is Suchihdram, about eight miles from Cape Comorin. Besides these, there are many lesser deities to whom homage is paid. There are temples and shrines dedicated to Ganesh and Subrahmaniya.[94]

In 1816, there were 19,524 Hindu temples of which 3,662 temples were dedicated to superior divinities, and 15,862 temples and groves were dedicated to inferior divinities.[95] Minor deities are known by the names of '*Madasami*' and '*karuppasami*'. Their spirit worship is known as *chavar* (literally death or dead). The spiritism and fetishism were in practice to protect the individual or communities from dangers or to safeguard them from the higher powers. Moreover, it was also the religion of hill tribes in Travancore particularly Kanikkars who were regarded as animists. They worshipped three kinds of deities such as spirits, minor divinities and superior divinities. Their worship was mainly to free the people from disease or starvation.[96]

4.2. Islam

It is believed that Muslims might have come in the 7th or 8th century itself as Arab traders. Gradually, the number of Muslims in South Travancore increased both by conversion and by the migration of Arab traders. The indigenous Muslims of South Travancore are generally called '*Jonaka* or *Chonaka Mappillas.*' Jonaka Mappilla constituted an important part of Muslim population. They were of foreign lineage, being descended from the Arabs. As an industrious community, their main occupation was trade. A few engaged in industry and agriculture. A vast majority of Muslims in Travancore concentrated in the province of Malabar. According to the census of 1891, there were 453 Mosques in Travancore. The Muslim priests

94 John A. Jacob, *A History of the London Missionary Society in South Travancore, 1806-1959*, 5.

95 C. M. Agur, *Church History of Travancore,* New Delhi: Asian Educational Service, 1990, 9.

96 V. Nagam Aiya, *The Travancore State Manual, Vol. 111,* 40.

were known under the name of '*Tangals*' and exercised a considerable influence over the Muslims.[97]

4.3. Christianity

Christians were a very significant minority in South Travancore. According to tradition, St. Thomas, one of the twelve apostles of Jesus Christ, brought Christianity to Travancore. However, there is a continuous history of Christianity at least from 4th century A.D. The ancient Christian Community is known as 'Thomas Christians' or 'Syrian Christians'. They ranked after the Brahmins and as equals of the Nairs. They engaged in trade and business and they received several privileges and favors at the hands of the ruling monarchs.[98] The arrival of Portuguese encouraged a large number of people from low castes to convert to Christianity. They were generally termed as 'Latin Christians'. A major section of Syrian Christians also joined the Catholic Church of the Portuguese.

4.4. Other Religions

Jainism, there is only one Jain temple existing in Travancore. About 4 miles north of Kuzhithurai in South Travancore, there is an interesting old temple situated on a huge rock known as Chitaral Rock Temple. The famous Hindu temple at Nagercoil is thought to have been originally a Jain temple. It has a shrine dedicated to '*Ananta*'- a serpent god. It was also believed that these Jain temples were taken by the Hindus and converted into Hindu Temples. The inscriptions found in these temples which date back to the 16th and 17th centuries refer to the gifts made to the 'Naga' and to the Naga Kings by two persons whose names resemble to Jain names.[99]

Judaism, according to tradition, the Jews came to Travancore in 68 A.D. in order to find a refuge after the destruction of their great temple at Jerusalem. They were confined to Cochin and Cranganore. The batches of Jewish immigrants came during subsequent years

---

97 V. Nagam Aiya, *The Travancore State Manual*, *Vol. II,* 110ff.

98 A. Sreed Bala Menm, *A Survey of Kerala History*, Kottayam: National Book Stall, 1970, 31.

99 John A. Jacob, *A History of the London Missionary Society in South Travancore, 1806-1959*, 6ff.

and laid the foundation of community life in this land. The Jewish settlers of Travancore made a good deal of economic prosperity by trade and commerce. They enjoyed certain rights and privileges from the rulers of Kerala. The Jews, both white and black neither inter-married nor made use of the same synagogue. Many of their manners and observances have close resemblances to that of the Hindus.[100]

Buddhism, the 1901 census shows that there were in Travancore only 227 Buddhists, 151 Jews, 15 Sikhs, 2 Parsis and only one Jain.[101] There was once a strong Buddhist influence in South Travancore. A figure was discovered at Pallikal and Chitaral, villages which come under Vilavancode Taluk of South Travancore. The temples at Chitaral and Pallikal, retained many of their Buddhist features. In 1881, the same temples were converted and dedicated to Goddess Bhagavati.[102]

Conclusion

The political context of Travancore in the end of 18th century can be considered as a period of the transition of power from the king to British East India Company. By the appointment of British Resident, the whole administrative system was directly or indirectly controlled by the East India Company as per treaty. Social structure of the society was based on caste system and religious laws. The high caste people enjoyed all the social privileges in the name of religion and social customs. The most unfortunate sections of the Travancore society were the so-called low caste people and slaves. Because of the socio-religious sanctions, they were illiterate and deprived of all rights. The low caste people faced oppression from the high caste people in all areas of life. The oppressive structure that prevailed in Travancore created a culture of inequality among the people of Travancore State. The heavy taxes and the evil systems of society like slavery, *pulapedi*, child marriage, etc., made the low caste people socially de-humanized and physically and economically weak. But these elements helped the high caste to enjoy the maximum benefits.

---

100 R.J. Hepzy Joy, *History and Development of Education of Women in Kerala*, 36.

101 V. Nagam Ayia, *The Travancore State Manual, Vol. 11*, 224.

102 V. Nagam Aiya, *The Travancore State Manual , Vol. 11*, 224.

The practices of child marriage and devadasi system tarnished the dignity of women, especially the low castes. Though the state was financially better because of trade, natural resources, agriculture and various taxes, the poor people were not benefited in the economic progress of the country. Rather they were burdened with many taxes and regulations. The presence of different religious groups before the arrival of missionary societies shows the religious tolerant approach of the Travancore rulers even though they had come as traders or as invaders. In this historical context, LMS missionaries came to spread the Gospel. But by seeing these social realities they involved in the affairs of people along with their assigned responsibilities. In short, the historical background of South Travancore was conducive for missionaries in all aspects.

Chapter 2

The London Missionary Society in South Travancore

Introduction

The history of Protestant Christianity in South Travancore is being closely associated with the need of the people living in South Travancore. The people of the land, the low caste people were politically, religiously, socially oppressed. The Protestant Missionaries were sent by its society to liberate the people from the bondage of prevailed evils in this region. The Mission viewed that the sending of the missionaries could some what ameliorate their condition of the people in South Travancore. The missionaries were sent to labour both for the temporal and spiritual welfare of the country. In the beginning, no missionary was inclined to make even a trial in South Travancore having been proposed with imaginary terrors about the country and the people and other excuses of a similar nature.[1] The Christian faith was brought to South Travancore by the Jesuit missionary, Francis Xavier in the 16th century. The Protestant Mission body LMS contributed much for the people of South Travancore

1 C.M. Agur, *Church History of Travancore*, New Delhi: Asian Educational Services, 1990, 471.

from the early 19th century. The LMS missionaries concentrated their work on church planting, health care, education, and social emancipation. This chapter concentrates on the mission activities of the LMS from 1806-947.

1. Christianity in South Travancore Before 1800 A.D

1.1. Roman Catholic Church

The Protestant Church in South Travancore is several centuries younger to the Roman Catholic Church. From the late thirteenth century onwards, emissaries of the western (Roman) Church and lay European travelers began to appear in India.[2] The Society of Jesus was founded by Ignatius of Loyola on 15th August 1534 with a commitment to chastity, poverty and obedience and to do mission work among the Muslims, and to subject them in absolute obedience to the Pope.[3] The Society of Jesus was formed to counter the Protestant reformation. As a movement, this encounter began in the 16th century with the missionary methods of unique personalities – the Jesuit missionaries namely Francis Xavier (1542 A.D.) and Robert de Nobili (1605 A.D.).[4] Robert de Nobili was known to the Madura mission for the adaptation method. The christianization of religious customs helped him to have few high caste people as a converts for Madura Mission.[5]

The depressed classes, the Paravas, who were fishermen, lived on the coastal areas of Travancore, Kanyakumari, Tuticorin and the areas extended up to the modern Gulf of Manaar. People of this region were exploited by the Muslims and to a very great extent suppressed by them. It was quite usual that troubles and fights with the Muslims

---

2 C. B. Firth, *An Introduction to Indian Church History*, Delhi: ISPCK, 1998, 37.

3 Aloysius Soares, *Catholic Church in India: A Historical Sketch*, Nagpur: Government Press and Book Depot, 1964, 62.

4 Dr. S. Padmanabhan, *Historic Churches in Kanyakumari*, Vol. V, Nagercoil, Aayvu Kalanjiam, December, 2003, 36, Refer, Stephen Neill, *A History of Christianity in India: The Beginning to AD 1707*, Cambridge, Cambridge University Press, 1984.

5 S. Raja Manickam, Robert *de Nobili and Adoptation*, Indian Church History Review, Vol. I/2, December 1967, Church History Association of India, Banglore, 83.

frightened Paravas. It was in these circumstances, the Paravas applied for assistance from the Portuguese authorities at Cochin by sending a number of their '*Patangatains*'.[6] It is recorded that, the Portuguese on the advice of Joam De Cruz routed the Muslims and gave the fishery coast back to the Paravas. Some priests were also sent among them, the chief was Miguel Vaz, the Bishop of Goa's vicariate. After the defeat of the Muslims, inhabitants of thirty villages became Christians. This "mass conversion" took place around 1536, and there were about nearly 10,000 christians before the arrival of Francis Xavier in South India. The missionary gathered the converts and formed them into congregations.[7]

To protect the Christians in south Travancore, Francis Xavier (1506-1552) was sent to India by the Society of Jesus to work among the 'Parava' converts, who lived on the South East coast opposite to Ceylon.[8] Francis Xavier and three Indian helpers traveled around the west coast where they found the Paravas living in thirty villages between Cape Comorin and Tuticorin. Francis Xavier learnt Tamil and translated the Creed, Ten Commandments, and Lord's Prayer into Tamil. He used the hand bell and by ringing it he was able to catch the attention of the people and began to teach the children of this town. He requested the children to teach their parents.[9] Therefore, the Christians of the coastal areas of Kanyakumari district rightly claim St. Francis Xavier as the apostle of their territory, which was known as the Travancore Coast.[10] The people of South Travancore believed that the prayers and support of St. Francis Xavier saved the Paravas of this region them from the hand of Vijayanagar army in the

---

6 Hendry James Colleridge, *The Life and Letters of St. Francis Xavier*, Vol. 1, London, 1874, 143ff. (Patangatains – Local chiefs or ambassadors)

7 Vicent K Kumaradoss, *Robert Caldwell, A Scholar- Missionary in Colonial South India*, ISPCK, Delhi, 2007, 35.

8 M. K. Kuriakose, *History of Christianity in India; Source Materials*, ISPCK, Delhi, 1982, 27.

9 Joseph Tekkadeth, *History of Christianity in India,* Vol. 1, Bangalore: CHAI, 1982, 166.

10 Joy Gnanadason, *A Forgotten History: The Story of the Missionary Movement and the Liberation of People in South Travancore,* Madras: Gurukul Lutheran Theological College and Research Institute, 1994, 46f.

time expedition to the South against Unni Kerala Varma, the king of Travancore.[11]

1.2. Protestant Mission in South Travancore

At the end of the 17th century the revival that broke out in Germany brought fresh missionary enthusiasm and evangelical awakening in England and America. As a result several missionary societies were formed. They viewed their task as essentially one of saving individual souls.[12] Prof. A H Francke of the University of Halle, Germany, gave a re-emphasis upon personal commitment. The evangelical awakening created a desire to share the personal experience with others, even in foreign lands, including India.[13] Lutherans were the pioneers in establishing Protestant mission stations in India.[14] The East India Company was directed by the Board of Directors, and on 5th September 1698 they appointed chaplains. On 9th July 1706, the first Protestant missionaries came to serve in India. Bartholomeaus Ziegenbalg and Heinrich Plutschau of Halle University in Germany were sent under the patronage of Frederick IV, the King of Denmark.[15] They arrived at Tranquebar and began their work by learning Portuguese and Tamil.[16] They established mission stations, churches, schools, orphanages and a printing industry.

---

11 Alin Suneja, *Letters of St. Francis Xavier as a Source for Sixteenth Century Tamilagam***,** Church History Review, Vol. XXXV/1, June 2001, Church History Assciation, Banglore, 67.

12 Johannes Verkuyl, *Contemporary Missiology*, Michigan: William B. Erdmans Publishing Company, 1975, 176.

13 Herbert Hoefer, *Debate on Mission*, Chennai: Gurukul Lutheran Theological and Research Institute, 1979, 39.

14 Bethval Powl, *Visvasathin Sathanai, C.S.I. Varalattu Pinnani*, (Tamil), Thiruchabaikalin samaya kalvikuzu Cheenai, 1996, 27.

15 Thomas Edmunds, *Tranquebar Missionaries and Three- Hundred Years of Lutheran Heritage: An Analysis*, Tercentenary Souvenir, Tamil Evangelical Lutheran Church, Tiruchirappalli: Best Offset, 2006.

16 C.B. Firth, *An Introduction to Indian Church History*, 132.

Ziegenbalg was an exceptionally talented man and within a short period, he translated the New Testament into Tamil.[17] Ziegenbalg translated Luther's Small Catechism, sermons, tracts, school books, the New Testament into Tamil and the Old Testament up to the book of Ruth. He studied Hinduism and wrote the '*Genealogy of Malabar Gods* and *Malabar Heathenism*'. A Tamil – German Dictionary was also compiled by him to develop the language skills of the people.[18] He started a school for the half native Portuguese in the year 1707 and in boarding schools, children were taught to read the Bible and Christian education was given much importance.[19] Ziegenbalg tolerated the prevailing caste system in the society and he realized the evil in the caste system but he believed that attack on caste system would cause more damage. So with a difference from the Catholics he tolerated caste.[20]

In England, the 'Society for Promoting Christian Knowledge'[21] had been formed in the year 1698 by the Anglican churches to spread Christian knowledge in the non-Christian lands.[22] The SPCK mission supported the Tranquebar mission and did evangelistic work in south Travancore. Evidences show that there were Christians belonging to the SPCK in South Travancore near Kanyakumari, before the LMS began to work under Ringeltaube.[23] Sathiyanathan, the Apostle of the Tinnevelly mission was instrumental for the missionaries work in this area with the help of David and the mission works were undertaken in Cape Comorin area. These Christians

---

17 B. Sobanan, *A History of the Christian Mission in South India, Trivandrum*, 1996, 159.

18 Peter Vedanayagamoni, *Introduction to History of Christianity in India*, Chennai: Hindustan Bible Institute, 59.

19 D. Arthur Jeyakumar, *History of Christianity in India: Selected Themes*, Delhi: SPCK, 2002, 29.

20 Peter Vedanayagamoni, *Introduction to History of Christianity in India*, 62.

21 Society for Promoting Christian Knowledge- cited hereafter as SPCK.

22 Joy Gnanadason, *A Forgotten History*, 47.

23 John A. Jacob, *A History of the London Missionary Society in South Travancore, 1806-1959*, 17.

suffered under persecution.[24] The SPCK missionaries had a cordial relationship with the Danish Missionaries in Tranquebar. The Evangelist, Sathiyanathan had worked in South Travancore from the year 1786 to 1805 and converted many people into Christian faith, particularly in the village Pichay- Kudiruppu (Kanyakumari).[25]

In his letter dated 15th December 1804, Rev. Sathiyanathan wrote to Rev. John Caspar Kohlhoff as follows: "On returning to Mudaloor, I sent Yesudian, Catechist, evangelist in a small village Church into Travancore. Yesudian reported that the Christians in Travancore were good people, and that country would not be in vain, but it was necessary to refrain from doing anything further just then."[26] For Bishop Caldwell, the Christian movement in Cape -Comorin began from an evangelist David.[27] At 1803, may be the Christians in South Travancore of this period might have died in famine.[28] It supports the argument that there were Christian converts by the SPCK missionaries in South Travancore. Though there was a mission work by SPCK, it was not able to establish mission stations in South Travancore.

2. The London Missionary Society

2.1. Origin

In 18th century, the social and religious life of England was in a deplorable condition and there was serious decline in moral standards. The established church showed a great lack of spiritual and social involvement. The Methodist Movement, however, showed a deep concern for the unprivileged people, which manifested itself

---

24 John A. Jacob, *A History of the London Missionary Society in South Travancore, 1806-1959,* 17.

25 John A. Jacob, *A History of the London Missionary Society in South Travancore, 1806-1959*, 15.

26 John A. Jacob, *A History of the London Missionary Society in South Travancore, 1806-1959*, 17.

27 F.J. Western, *The Early History of the Tinnavelly Church,* London: Oxford University Press, 1938, 89.

28 William Robinson, *Ringeltaube, the Rishi*, Sheffield: The Sheffield Independent Press Ltd, 1902, 99.

in a large number of charitable activities like starting schools and hospitals.[29] This evangelical awaking spread through out the world in the 19th century which was recognized as a great period of missionary expansion.[30] During this century British and American missions had an increasing and predominating share in world evangelization. In England new societies, namely the Baptist Missionary Society (1792), the London Missionary Society (1795), the Church Missionary Society (1799), and Methodist Missionary Society (1818) were formed and became the agencies of mission work in various countries. The London Missionary Society started its mission in South Travancore in 1806.[31]

The LMS was a non-denominational missionary society formed in England in 1795.[32] It was a letter by William Carey, written soon after he landed in India which provided the spark for the tinder. The letter was addressed in 1794 to John Ryland of Bristol, a minister of the Broadmead Church and President of the Baptist College. In response to this letter a small group of ministers came together and prepared themselves in prayer to strengthen the missionary concern of William Carey.[33] The result was that eight pastors came together and formed a Missionary Society on 21st September, 1795.[34] The original title of the London Missionary Society was simply "The Missionary Society". The name London was prefixed in 1818, as some confusion had arisen, and for want of a title more distinctive than which was adopted in 1795. Twenty five people served as the members of this

---

29 Dick Kooiman, "Social and Economic Backgrounds of 19th Century London Missionary Society in South Travancore", in Indian *Church History Review*, Vol. XIX, No. 11, December, 1985, 99.

30 Latourette, K.S, *A History of Expansion of Christianity*, Vol, IV, New York: Harper & Brothers Publishers, 1944, 3.

31 Norman Goodall, *A History of the London Missionary Society, 1895-1945*, London: Oxford University Press, 1954, 2.

32 John A. Jacob, *A History of the London Missionary Society in South Travancore, 1806-1959*, 17.

33 Norman Goodall, *A History of the London Missionary Society, 1895-1945*, 3.

34 Samuel Zachariah, *A Summery of the History of the Church in South Travancore, 1805-1855* (Tamil), Vol. I, Nagercoil: Mission Press, 1897, 2.

Society and they were from Congregational, Anglican, Presbyterian, and Wesleyan Methodist.[35]

The fundamental principle of the LMS is stated as the union of Christians of various denominations in carrying the Gospel of Jesus Christ to the non- Christian world. It was not to send Presbyterianism, Independency, Episcopacy or any other form of church order but the Gospel to the people of other religions.[36] The society did not like to form any kind of church government or order of the church. The Society believed that committed people should appear most agreeable to the word of God.[37] The fundamental principle of the LMS was added to the Society's bylaws in 1796.[38]

The first enterprise, upon which the LMS entered immediately after its establishment by sending the missionary ship "The Duff", under the leadership of Captain Wilson, carried 30 missionaries to the South Seas - 4 of them being ordained ministers, 25 artisans and one surgeon.[39] The first missionary of the LMS. in India was Rev. Nathaniel Forsyth, who came in the first instance to Calcutta, but finally settled in Chinsura, about 20 miles north of that city, because of the opposition of the East India Company. The Society's desire to send missionaries to South India- to the Tamil and Telugu areas in particular, was aroused by the invitations received from eminent missionaries of the Danish Mission in Tranquebar.[40] The LMS was the first Protestant organization to attempt proselytism in South Travancore and the mission started its work in 1806.[41]

---

35 Bethval Powl, *Visvasathin Sathanai, C.S.I. Varalattu Pinnani*, 63.

36 Beaver, R.P, *Ecumenical Beginning of the Protestant World Mission*, Thomas Nelson and sons, New York: USA, 1962, 20f.

37 *One Hundred and Thirty third Report of the LMS*, 1928, 23.

38 Norman Goodall, *A History of the London Missionary Society, 1895-1945*, 3.

39 John. A. Jacob, *A History of the London Missionary Society in South Travancore 1806-1959*, 19.

40 John A. Jacob, *A History of the London Missionary Society in South Travancore, 1806-1959*, 20.

41 T.K. Vellu Pillai, *The Travancore State* Manual, Vol. IV, Trivandrum: Travancore Press, 1940, 77.

2.2. The Selection of the First Missionary

As a result of the modern missionary movement in England, in the early 18th century, India became the field for mission work and 1805-1947 was known as period of the history of its mission in India.[42] Based on the request of Danish Mission in Tranquebar- on 20th April 1804, a party of 6 missionaries sent out to establish mission stations in South India and Ceylon. The ultimate decision of the particular places of the work was very wisely left to the missionaries themselves, who were at liberty to set as seemed best, with the advice of Christian friends on the spot and the guidance of God. The names of the missionaries were Rev. William Tobias Ringeltaube, Desgranges, Cran, Voss, Erhardt and Palm. They sailed from Copenhagen to Tranquebar in the Danish ship, "King's Packet" in April 1804.[43] Rev. William Tobias Ringeltaube[44] was interested to take part in the Church of England and became the rector of St. Mary Woolnoth. He was the pillar of the evangelical party in the Church of England,[45] was also to be called the first protestant LMS Missionary to South Travancore.[46] In 1803, LMS chose him and decided to send him to

---

42 C.M. Agur, *Church History of Travancore*, 464.

43 John A. Jacob, *A History of the London Missionary Society in South Travancore, 1806-1959*, 21.

44 William Tobias Ringeltaube was born on 8th August, 1770, as the first child to Gottlieb Ringeltaube; the vicar of Scheidelweltz, Brieg, He was impressed by the life of John Newton, who worked with slave trade in Africa. His desire was to become a missionary to the 'heathen'. He studied Theology at Halle University, Germany. When London Missionary Society made known its intention of sending out missionaries to India, Ringeltaube offered himself and was accepted. India was not a strange country to this young man as he had already spent a year as a missionary of the SPCK in Calcutta. The SPCK selected him as a minister for the English congregation at Calcutta and he was ordained on 24th July 1796, and arrived at Calcutta in Oct, 1797. He remained in Calcutta for one year and returned to England and joined the Moravians (Joy Gnanadoson, *A Forgotten History*, 52, William Robinson, *Ringeltaube, the Rishi*, 17).

45 Philip Schoff, *Religious Encyclopedia of Dictionary, Biblical, Historical, Doctrinal, and Practical Theology*, Vol. 11, Edinburgh: T &T Clark, 1883, 1641.

46 N. Martin Daniel Dhas. *Missionary Medical Work in Travancore, 1838-1958*, Marthandam: South India Press, 1985, 1.

Ceylon. He started on 10th April 1804 and reached at the flourishing Danish trading port Tharangampadi on the South East Coast of India on 5th December 1804. He spent some time in Tharangampadi and studied Tamil to work among the Tamil speaking people.[47]

3. The LMS in South Travancore

3.1. Beginning of the Mission (1806 to 1816)

Missionary Ringeltaube came to Tranquebar, the Danish Mission station and was directed to Tanjore and South Travancore.[48] Rev. John Caspar Kohlhoff's, working in Tanjore requested Ringeltaube to work among the Christians in Trinelveli.[49] Bishop Robert Caldwell, affirm the willingness of Ringeltaube by quoting the letter written by him to the Treasurer of the LMS on 5th August, 1805, that says,

> I intend, God willing to go to the South before the rainy season sets in. The mission cannot be so well carried on in great towns where Europeans reside as they sometimes counteract the pious labours of the missionary; I could not make up my mind to go to Madras or Seringapatam. But lately a man from Travancore came to me and begs I would come down and help them...It struck me as a call from God.[50]

It was believed that in this period 'Vethamanickam',[51] requested Rev. J. C. Kohlhoff for a missionary. In response Rev. J. C. Kohlhoff told him that a missionary named Ringeltaube had arrived from

---

47 Joy Gnanadoson, *A Forgotten History*, 52.

48 John A. Jacob, *A History of the London Missionary Society in South Travancore, 1806-1959*, Nagercoil: The Diocesan Press, 1990, 22.

49 C.B. Firth, *An Introduction to Indian Church History*, 206.

50 Caldwell Robert, *Records of the Early History of the Trinelvelli Mission of the SPCK and SPG*, Madras: Higginbothan & Co, 1881, 135f.

51 Vedamanickam was the first convert from South Travancore. His original name was Maharasan. He and his nephew Sivagurunadhan went on a Pilgrimage to Chidambaram. On their way back from Chidambaram they attended to a Sermon preached by Rev. Kohlhoff and accepted the new faith as well as received baptism from him with the new names of Vedamanickam and Masilamoni, respectively.

Europe and was learning Tamil in 'Tranquebar'.[52] He had been proposed that he should proceed to Vethamanickam village, Mylaudy.[53] Vethamanickam went and invited Ringeltaube to come and start the mission work in South Travancore.

Ringeltaube came to Mylaudy to see the forty families of the converts and went to Cochin to pay his respects to the British Resident, Colonel Macaulay. He also requested the British Resident to grant permission to build a Church at Mylaudy. The Resident asked him to speak to the Dewan. On 15th May 1806, on his way back he met the Dewan at Quilon, the seat of government. The request made to Dewan Velu Thampi was not accepted and with disappointment, he went to Palayamkottai and concentrated his work in the Tirunelveli District. Ringeltaube stayed in Tranquebar for several months, assisting the venerable Dr. John, the senior missionary of Tranquebar Mission, learning various branches of knowledge.[54] It was at this time that Vethamanickam was sent by Kohlhoff to Tranquebar. Kohlhoff's letter of introduction about Ringeltaube helped Vethamanickam to invite the missionary Ringeltaube to Travancore.[55] Ringeltaube was waiting for a providential opening. Ringeltaube's attention was directed to the Nadars in South Travancore.[56] Ringeltaube wrote to Colonel Macaulay, the British Resident in Travancore and requested for an official sanctioning from the Travancore Government. The British Resident Macaulay sanctioned permission and also came forward to convene the expenses for his journey.[57] On 1st March

---

52 There is a discrepancy among the authors about the place where Ringeltaube and Vedamanicam met for the first time. Robinson says they met at Madras (William Robinson, *Ringeltaube, The Rishi*, 94 and Bishop Caldwell the meeting took place at Tranquebar Caldwell Robert, *Records of the Early History of the Trinelvelli,* 130).

53 R.D. Paul, *Triumphs of Grace*, Madras: CLS, 1967, 59.

54 C.M. Agur, *Church History of Travancore*, 468.

55 C.M. Agur, *Church History of Travancore*, 469.

56 John A. Jacob, *A History of the London Missionary Society in South Travancore, 1806-1959,* 27.

57 John A. Jacob, *A History of the London Missionary Society in South Travancore, 1806-1959,* 29.

1807, Ringeltaube passed through Arambozhi (in South Travancore) Gate and arrived at Mylaudy.[58]

Ringeltaube came to Mylaudy the second time on the 1st March 1807, a year later to begin his mission. He came from Tranquebar to South Travancore with a well-planned programme of missionary methods.[59] The mission activities were based on his ten-point action plan.[60] He preached to the Christians assembled in a courtyard, under the open starry sky. They heard and agreed to his preaching wholeheartedly and he baptized 40 of them. In 1808 Dewan Velu Thampi started the open revolt against Christians. This was followed by the Travancore rebellion of 1809. The war affected the Christians of Mylaudy.[61] Travancore troops captured the Arambozhi fort. After three days Dewan collected his troops and waged war against the

58 John A. Jacob, *A History of the London Missionary Society in South Travancore, 1806-1959*, 33.

59 Joy Gnanadason, *A Forgotten History*, 55.

60 Ten Points action plan:
1. A mission should be established and a Church planted near the southern frontiers of Travancore, a sum of 10,000 pounds being required to purchase land and erect the necessary buildings. 2. Twelve young men should be chosen from the existing churches and formed into a Boarding School and each youth would require one and a half star pagodas or Rs. 6 per month. 3. As soon as their course in the school was over, these young men should be sent out two by two as itinerant preachers on a salary of two stars pagodas each. 4. Those among them who found real grace and proved worthy of their calling should be ordained as ministers, after a solemn pledge from them, they would do their pastoral duty to the entire satisfaction of the congregation. 5. They should annually meet in council presided over by a European missionary as they would thereby derive much knowledge and wisdom to lead and control churches, which is greatly wanting among the present catechists. 6. If a particular congregation desires the service of any pastor, on promise of supporting him, he should be sent to them. 7. Together with such benevolent institutions a printing press should be established. 8. Those who show real repentance of their sins and believe in the Lord Jesus Christ should be baptized. 9. Communion should be established by giving often the sacrament of the Lord's Supper only to those who really convert. 10. To carry on the work of the mission on the above scheme, a sum of Rs. 2,000/- or 200 pounds would be annually required (C. M. Agur, *Church History of Travancore*, 509-510).

61 Samuel Zechariah, *A Summery of the History of the Church in South Travancore, 1805-1855*, 11.

Travancore troops at Ozhugunasery near Nagercoil. But the troops of Dewan failed and they ran away from the battlefield and went to the fort Padmanabhapuram to plunder many precious things.[62] Vethamanickam, the follower of the white man and friend of the Resident was a marked man. Orders were given to seize and imprison him or shoot him at sight. He and the members of his family took shelter in the nearby Maruthuvazhe Hills for about 30 days.[63] Ringeltaube fled to Tirunelveli and kept away from the Travancore borders. During the year 1810 to 1812 he stayed at Udayagri conducting worship for Europeans. People from Amandivilai, Anandhanadarkudy, Peyankuzi, Moolachi, and Mathicode went to Udayagri and they were baptized by him.[64] The armies of the Raja were defeated and Velu Thampy committed suicide. Then Ringeltaube returned to Mylaudy.[65] He settled at Mylaudy, the village of Vethamanickam where he founded the first Protestant Church of Travancore in the year 1809, after getting Government permission with great difficulty.[66] When Ringeltaube, the Protestant Missionary requested Col. Macaulay for a permit to travel through the territories of Travancore, Col. Macaulay not only secured him the permit, but also contributed from his own purse money to defray the expenses of the journey. He was the first in a succession of British representatives who utilized their official position for spreading the faith.[67]

The first church and school were built in Mylaudy at the end of the year 1809. From here the Gospel began to spread to the near by villages. Ringeltaube traveled from village to village and at certain fixed centers held baptismal services and administered the Holy Sacraments.[68] After 12 years of labour in South India, he became weak

---

62 Samuel Zechariah, *A Summery of the History of the Church in South Travancore, 1805-1855*, 12.

63 Samuel Zechariah, *A Summery of the History of the Church in South Travancore, 1805-1855*, 13.

64 John A. Jacob, *Triple Jubilee Commemoration*, Volume 20th Aug, 1956, Nagercoil: London Mission Press, 1956, 31.

65 Joy Gnanadasan, *A Forgotten History*, 57.

66 Martin Daniel Dhas, *Missionary Medical Work in Travancore, 1838-1958*, 2.

67 T.K. Vellu Pillai, *The Travancore State Manual*, Vol. I, 725.

68 Joy Gnanadason, *A Forgotten History,* 57ff.

and during 1814 and 1815 his health seemed steadily to decline. He requested the LMS to send another missionary and Ringeltaube did not receive positive response from the Society. Therefore he ordained the native of this region, Vethamanickam and appointed him as his successor. After bidding good-bye to Colonel Munro and his good lady, he left the shores of Travancore from the port of Quilon on 5th February, 1816. He was last heard of from Malacca.[69] Ringeltaube had established mission on a very firm foundation.[70] He was followed by a total of 48 LMS men and two lady missionaries who became part of mission work in South Travancore.[71] The LMS missionaries who came after him served along with the native, Vethamanickam in South Travancore.

The beginning of Protestant Christianity South Travancore is related with the personal history of Vethamanickam, whose name was Maha Rasan.[72] He worked with the missionary Ringeltaube in Mylaudy and Kottaram and other neighboring villages. Ringeltaube gave the mission responsibilities to him when he left the mission station

69 Joy Gnanadoson, *A Forgotten History*, 61.

70 R.J. Hepzy Joy, *History and Development of Education of Women in Kerala*, 61.

71 Dick Kooiman, *Conversion and Social Equality in India*, New Delhi: Manohar, 1989, 35.

72 He was an orthodox Saivite Hindu lived in the little village of Mylaudy about four and a half kilometers North East of the Cape Comorin (Kanyakumari). He belonged to a caste that was called as Harijans by Gandhi and later recognized as a scheduled caste by the government of India in the year 1935. His ancestors were from Tanjore then came Trinelveli and in later time came and settled in Myladi. He went on a pilgrimage to Chidambaram, the holiest of the Sevivite Shrines in South India. He went there hoping to find the peace of mind and rest for his soul which he had long been seeking. At Chidambaram his inner longings were not satisfied rather he was offended with the sight he saw. He started the journey back in accordance with the dream which he had and on the way he met some Christians as well as missionaries at Tanjore. He returned home as a Christian with a new name Vethamanickam. He was soon able to make relatives and friends to see the new light and formed a small group of Christians. In all about thirty persons professed Christianity publicly and put them under Vethamanickam's instructions (C. M. Agur, *Church History of Travancore*, 424; Joy Gnanadason, *A Forgotten History*, 42; John A. Jacob, 24; R.D. Paul, *Neelakandan Devadasan*, Madras: CLS, 1971, 5; R.D. Paul, *Triumphs of His Grace*, Madras: CLS, 1967, 58).

to his mother land. This shows the faithfulness of his committed work for the people of south Travancore. The people of South Travancore were very pleased with his preaching. Vethamanickam used Hindu terminology in his evangelization method. He held the Tamil New Testament in his hand and said, this is the true *Prasatham*, the true *Vibuth*i, this is the heavenly bread sent to us by the King of Kings as the gift of God. Though people had the message from the SPCK missionaries, this was the first experience to hear the word of God from a native Christian evangelist. The people of the South Travancore wondered at the gracious words of Vethamanickam.[73] The leaders of the Hindu community made persistent attempts to stop its spread. Even the Government officials who were mainly from the Nair Hindu community did not tolerate the coming of a new religion to South Travancore.[74] Vethamanickam wanted to sell the lands and move to Tanjore because of the disturbances faced from the Hindus. In this time Vethamanickam received information from Rev. John Caspar Kohlhoff' about the arrival of new missionaries in Tranquebar. Then he changed his mind and went to Tanjoure to see the missionaries.[75] They went again to Tharangampadi and requested Rev. Kohlhoff to send a missionary to Travancore. He and his brother Gnanamuthu offered their own lands for the church building. He converted the people to the new faith and changed their old names at the time of baptism.[76] Vethamanickam was ordained to priesthood and was given authority to minister till the Society sent another missionary to take over.[77] He was an ably assisted by his nephew Masillamony, his eldest son Devasagayam, his son-in-law Pakkianathen, and other

73 C.M. Agur, *Church History of Travancore*, 447.

74 William Robinson, *Ringeltaube, The Rishi*, 57.

75 William Robinson, *Ringeltaube, The Rishi,* 58.

76 To differentiate the people of new faith, in the time of Baptism new names were given, Vethamanickam's wife was named as Sathiyathai, daughters - Pakiyai, Annamal, son - Devasgayam and some other women - Yesuvadiyal, Santhayi, Annanthayi, Mariyal, men were- Joseppu, Gnanamuthu, Pakiyanathan. This practice continued in the present churches of South Travancore up to the middle of 20th century that the converts from other faith were baptized with new names (Samuel Zachariah, 6).

77 Joy Gnanadasson, *A Forgotten History*, 62.

members of the family.[78] In their period (1806 to 1816) of work the mission was able to open seven churches and a school with thirty two students.[79] Ringeltaube and Vethamanickam were the pioneers of LMS in establishing the mission work in South Travancore.

3.2. The Development of the Mission (1817-1860)

During this period Charles Mead, Charles Mault, Dr. Ramsay and few other LMS missionaries came and developed the mission work that was established by the pioneer missionary Ringeltaube in South Travancore. Charles Mead[80] purchased few acres of land from Pavanasadavar and gave the same to the poor Christian immigrants who were willing to settle at Nagercoil. He extended much help

---

78 I.H. Hacker, *A Hundred Years in Travancore,* London: H.R. Allenson Limited, 31.

79 G. Christdhas, *Paathachuvadukal,* 557.

80 Charles Mead (1817 to 1853) was born on 1st October 1792 at Bristol, Glouccestershire in England. He lost his parents very early and was brought up under the sole guidance and management of his uncle Rev. John Hunt of the Church of England in London. He prosecuted his studies in a Grammer School till he accepted the invitation of the LMS. Mead was one of the four young men admitted by the Missionary Society in 1814 who had previously received the rudiments of a learned education. While preparing to set out for India, Mead married Ann Hunt, daughter of his uncle John Hunt. He took voyage to the East and landed Madras on 28th August 1816. His wife died on the ship and had a child. Then the father and the child took voyage to Travancore to be landed at Colachel in December 1817. Thus Mead reached Travancore by the beginning of 1818 to take charge of the young Mylaudy Mission as left by Ringeltaube. He was not having a convenient house in Maylaudy for his comfortable stay. Therefore, Mead transferred his Headquarters from Mylaudy to Nagercoil. After the retirement of Mead in 1853 the Neyyoor press was moved to Nagercoil. The Nagercoil and Neyyoor Religious Tract Societies were united under the title "The South Travancore Tract and Book Society". Mead lived up to the age of 82. He passed away on 19th January 1873 and was buried in the Christ Church Cemetery Trivandrum. His three sons Theodere, Knill and Joseph died in the years 1830, 1836, 1832 and were buried in Neyoor. Mrs. Mead was attacked by liver complaint which terminated rapidly in her death. She died at Neyyoor on 6th February 1845 at the age of 45. (Samuel Zechariah, *A Summery of the History of the Church in South Travancore, 1805-1855,* 35 & John Owen White House, Register of Missionaries Deputations, London, London Missionary Society, 36 ; C.M. Agur, 758).

towards the erection of their small houses.[81] He was appointment as Judge of the Nagercoil Court by the Government of Travancore in 1818. The Maharani gave the Resident's Camp Bungalow in Nagercoil as a gift to the Mission and Mead moved to Nagercoil in April 1818.[82] In 1818 a social transformation gathered momentum among the Nadars of South Travancore. This was mainly due to the extension of English education and other job – oriented training programmes in spinning, knitting, sewing, lace-making and embroidery, and other domestic work for girls. For Boys, instruction was imparted on teaching, printing, tailoring, book binding, tanning and other arts. Neyyoor and Nagercoil became the centers of all types of education and Mission work.[83] For educating the Christian and Hindu youths Charles Mead opened a Seminary or Boarding School for boys in October 1819.[84] He set up a Printing press in Nagercoil which according to him was "valuable but necessary appendage to a Missionary Establishment". This press was the first printing press in Travancore.[85] In 1819, Mead married Johanna Coclestina Horyst. She helped Mead to establish a 'Central School' or Seminary for Boys at Nagercoil.[86] Mead's main aim was to increase the revenue of the Mission and to give work to the families of the poor Christians. Accordingly he converted waste lands into paddy fields yielding a fairly good produce.[87] Mead built a Chapel at Kotanarvillay in 1822.[88] Mead and his wife helped many Christians to come and settle there. Mead also helped five Pulaya families to settle at Neyyoor and gave them lands for cultivation.[89]

---

81 C.M. Agur, *Church History of Travancore*, 679f.

82 Joy Gnanadasan, *A Forgotten History*, 68.

83 D. Daniel, *Travancore Tamils Struggle for Identity, 1938-1956*, Raj Publishers Madurai, 1983, 10.

84 R.N. Yesudas, *A People's Revolt in Travancore: A Background Movement for Social Freedom*, Kerala Historical Society, Manju Publishing House, Trivandrum, 1975, 65.

85 R.N. Yesudas, *A People's Revolt in Travancore*, 69.

86 Joy Gnanadasan, *A Forgotten History*, 69.

87 C.M. Agur, *Church History of Travancore*, 695.

88 C.M. Agur, *Church History of Travancore*, 734.

89 D. Daniel, *Travancore Tamils Struggle for Identity, 1938-1956*, 6.

Charles Mault.[90] He was Missionary of extra ordinary labour in the Nagercoil Mission.[91] In 1819 the LMS sent Rev. Charles Mault and Mrs. Mault to Travancore.[92] He helped Mead to establish a Seminary School at Nagercoil.[93] The school started by Ringeltaube was upgraded as a seminary in 1819 and Mrs. Mead and Mrs. Mault joined together and started a boarding school in 1820. They also implemented lace production to meet the expenses for the school going girls.[94] Mead and Mault wrote for the need of Press to the Mission body and they were able to get it in 1820. In 1820 the printing work started at Nagercoil.[95] Following his death, his co-worker Richard Knill[96] assumed the responsibility.

---

90 Charles Mault (1819 to 1858), was born on 11th may 1791, church member of St. Neot's, studied at Neot's , married to Martha on 24th Oct 1818, sailed on 10th Dec, 1818 and reached Bombay on 18th May 1819, served in South Travancore as a LMS missionary from 1819-1885. He did not, however, long enjoy his retirement. He died of stroke on 17th October 1858 and was buried in the local cemetery (C.M. Agur, *Church History of Travancore*, 914).

91 John Owen White House, *Register of Missionaries Deputations*, London: London Missionary Society, 1896, 52.

92 Samuel Zechariah, *A Summery of the History of the Church in South Travancore, 1805-1855*, 75.

93 Samuel Zechariah, *A Summery of the History of the Church in South Travancore, 1805-1855*, 75.

94 John A. Jacob, *Triple Jubilee Commemoration Volume*, Nagarcoil: The Diocesan Printing Press, 1990, 38f.

95 John A. Jacob, *Triple Jubilee Commemoration Volume*, 39.

96 Richard Knill (1818-1819) was born on April 14, 1787 at Braunton in England. He was the younger child of his mother. He sailed with Mead from England was posted to Madras. Very soon he had to leave that town owing to ill health and before he left for England he was invited to Travancore by Mr. Mead. Responding the invitation Knill reached Travancore in September 1818. Altogether he worked only two years in India and thirty eight years in England and Russia. Having rendered service to the cause of the Mission in different countries Knill died on 2nd January 1857 at his age of seventy. Charles Mead and Richard Knill had an idea to construct a Church at Nagercoil and started its work in 1819. When Mead and Knill were thus actively engaged, their important labours went much obstructed by a fearful visitation of Cholera which desolated the Southern parts of Travancore. Knill stayed with Mr. Mead in Travancore only for about five months from September 1818 to

Rev. John Smith[97] was sent by the Mission Society to work with Mead and Mault.[98] Mead and Mault served together for almost forty years in south Travancore concentrating on Nagercoil and Neyyoor mission work respectively.[99] In 1824 the mission was having 48 churches and 47 schools and the number of Christians increased rapidly.[100] The missionaries William Miller,[101] Charles Miller[102] came

---

15th February 1819. (C.M. Agur, *Church History of Travancore, 709,* Samuuel Zechariah, *A Summery of the History of the Church in South Travancore, 1805-1855,* 66).

97 Rev. John Smith: arrived at Nagercoil on 16th February 1820. He stayed one year with Mead and Mault where he was chiefly engaged in learning the vernacular and spent his leisure moments in supervising the building of the Nagercoil Church. As he had a particular training in carpentry he instructed the native carpenters of Kottar who were engaged in the work (C.M. Agur, *Church History of Travancore,* 710).

98 C.M. Agur, *Church History of Travancore,* 752f.

99 John A. Jacob, *Triple Jubilee Commemoration Volume*, 37.

100 John A. Jacob, *A History of the London Missionary Society in Travancore*, 69.

101 William Miller (1828-1838) was born on 1st Dec, 1804 at Thurso, studied at Gosport and missionary college Hoxton and was ordained on 8th Feb, 1827 at Queen's street chapel, Leeds. His wife was Mary Pitman, church member of Portsea. He was appointed as a missionary to South Travancore and sailed with his wife on 10th April, 1827 and arrived in Madras on 5th August and Nagercoil on 31st Oct, 1827. His first wife died at Nagercoil on 21st January 1828. He married Sophia Eusebia Horst. At Madras the deputation met and welcomed three new missionaries for Travancore. William Miller was placed to help Mead in Nagercoil. Mainly he worked hard for the extension of mission work Neyyoor. He died on 24th April, 1838 in Nagercoil (John Owen White House, 75, John A .Jacob, *Triple Jubilee Commemoration* Volume, 54).

102 Charles Miller (1833-1841) born in the year 1805 at Forfar, studied at Edinburg. Ordained to priesthood, on 29th May 1833 at Albion Chapel, London, married in India on 15th March, 1836. His wife died at Neyyoor on 22nd May 1837. He died in Poonamallee on 9th September, 1842. Charles Miller was appointed by the Mission Society to South Travancore. He reached Madras on 5th October, 1833. He was placed in Neyyoor. He was the first purely educational missionary in the mission; and also holding the responsibility of the Seminary at Nagercoil. He worked hard still his death. He served both in Neyyoor and Nagercoil for seven years (I.H. Hacker, *A Hundred Years in Travancore* 39. John Owen Whitehouse, 85, Samuel Zechariah, *A Summery of the History of the Church in South Travancore, 1805-1855, Vol. 1,* 199).

and served both in Nagercoil and Neyyoor mission places in South Travancore. The printing press was introduced by the missionaries and the printing work began in the year 1830.[103] At that time the mission area was divided into two Mission Districts,[104] namely Nagercoil and Neyyoor.

Dr. Ramsay (1838 to 1842) was the first Medical missionary to South Travancore and was also the second medical missionary ever sent forth from England by the Society. He started his medical work in Nagercoil. A small hospital was erected, but in 1842 he left the mission for other work, and for ten years people of this region suffered much for their medical treatment.[105] The treatment was made possible to all the people irrespective of caste and creed. The medical work was also supported by Indians particularly of other religious faiths and it was reported that within three months about 1500 got medical treatment.[106] John Cox[107] came and served in Neyyoor mission areas of Colachel and Mathicode. John Abbs[108] and

---

103 John A. Jacob, *A History of the London Missionary Society in Travancore, 72.*

104 Mission District: When the churches were increased in South Travancore the missionaries divided the LMS field into many parts that was called as mission districts. Each mission district had a head quarter and a missionary would be the charge of mission district.

105 I.H. Hacker, *A Hundred Years in Travancore.* 41.

106 John A. Jacob, *Triple Jubilee Commemoration* Volume, 60.

107 John Cox (1838-1861) was a man of unusual energy and independence of character. He entered on his work and carried it forward with great ardor. John Cox: born in the year 1811 at Painswick, Gloucestershire, studied in Highbury College. Ordained at Stroud on 27th July 1837 sailed on 20th October, 1837 and reached Quilon on 31st March, 1838. He left an enduring mark upon the annals of the mission. He was appointed to South Travancore and came to Neyyoor on 20th April, 1838. He look after the mission work in the places namely Mathicode, Colachel, that were the mission stations belong to the Neyyoor District. In 1848 returned to England and then returned to India on 20th July, 1851. In 1861 he resigned his connection with the society but continues to be residing in South Travancore and was died in Neyyoor on 23rd March, 1895 (John Owen White House, 107).

108 John Abbs (1838-1845) was born on December 20th, 1810 at Norwich, educated from Cheshunt College. He was ordained on August, 23rd 1837. His wife was Louisa Sewell Skipper. He retired from Foreign Service in 1861 and was a Priest at Kirby Moorside, Yorkshire. His wife died on June 25th 1877.

James Russel[109] worked as the LMS missionaries in Nagercoil and Neyyoor mission districts.

In this period mission he went to the stage of starting schools at almost all the stations of their mission fields. The mission began to concentrate on people's health for which medical missionaries were sent by the Mission Board and the missionaries started their health care work in South Travancore. In 1860's schools were functioning in almost all the mission stations. There were 84 village schools, 25 schools for girls in Nagercoil and Neyoor, two boarding schools at Nagercoil and Neyoor, and three boarding schools for girls in Nagercoil, Neyoor and Santhapuram. To educate the ordinary farmers and workers the mission had 17 night schools.[110]

3.3. Further Development (1861 to 1890)

John Owen Whitehouse[111] served seventeen years. He was in charge of the Seminary, printing press and Nagercoil mission district. He

---

He resigned his pastorate in 1877 and died at Kirby Moorside on March 19th, 1888. John Abbs was appointed to South Travancore by the Mission Society and sailed to India on October 20th and arrived at Quilon on March 31st, and reached Neyyoor on April 20th 1837. He took charge of the Neyyoor mission and resided in Neyyoor until 1845. (I.H. Hacker, *A Hundred Years in Travancore*, 41).

109 James Russell (1840-1860) was appointed as a missionary to the Eastern part of the Nagercoil and he formed a new mission station in the place called James Town. He served there for almost twenty years. He was in charge of twenty churches. The native workers namely Devadason, Masillamoni and Devasagayam were served him as evangelists. A beautiful church and a school were constructed, and presently the school is functioning as Higher Secondary School (I.H. Hacker., *A Hundred Years in Travancore,* 41).

110 Dr. S.S Hector, *Then Thiruvithankooril Protestanat Missionkalin Samuthaya Vallarchiahal, (Tamil- The Growth of Protestant in South Travancore),*Church of South India, Kanyakumari Diocese Souvenir 2006, 155.

111 John Owen Whitehouse (1842 to 1861) was born on 23rd April 1815 at Dorking, educated from Cheshunt College, and was ordained to priesthood on 8th June 1842 at the Weigh House Chapel. He married Sarah Mault in India on 9th January 1849. She died on 30th June 1861. He joined the Society as the director from April 30th 1875. The book, '*Register of the missionaries of the society*' was compiled by him and was printed in 1877. He was appointed as a missionary to South Travancore. Sailed to India on 26th June, 1842 and arrived

taught his students regularly Systematic Theology, side by side with other studies. He also instituted a system of annual examinations for the improvement of catechists.[112] From 1856 because of Lewis' departure he was given charge of Santhapuram mission work. From June 1856 due to James Russel's visit to Australia, the James Town Mission work was also added to his work. Mrs. John Owen White house became sick which forced him to return to England and after that he never came back to India. His connection with the Society ceased on 30th July 1861.[113] He stood as an example for evangelistic work and the improvement of elementary education in Tamil language. Ebenezer Lewis (1846-1881) served in Nagercoil and John Joll Dennis[114] worked for the mission in Neyyoor.

---

in Madras on September 22nd, 1842. His arrival to Nagercoil mission district was on November15th, 1842. In January 9th, 1843 he took the responsibility of superintendence to the Travancore mission seminary. (John, Owen White House, *Register of Missionaries Deputations*, 144ff).

112 John A Jacob, *Triple Jubilee Commemoration Volume*, 65.

113 John Owen White House, *Register of Missionaries Deputations*, 145.

114 John Joll Dennis (1856-1864) was permanently appointed to succeed Mr. Mault at Nagercoil. Dennis arrived in February 1856. He was especially skilled in printing work. He took the mission charge of Nagercoil district and turned it into good account in Travancore. Due to his wife illness he went back to England in 1864 and returned in the same year and died on 15th Nov 1864 was buried in Nagercoil cemetery (C.M. Agur, 915).

Fredrick Baylis,[115] came to Neyyoor and served as an active agent of the gospel.[116]

Leitch Charles Calder[117] was working as a medical missionary. After the resignation of Mead from his mission work, he was given

---

115 Baylis Fredrick (1850-1877) born on 18th November 1825 at Rodborough, Gloucestershire was educated from Rotherham College. He was appointed as a missionary to South Travancore. He and his wife Eliza Ann White sailed to India on 14th September 1850 and reached Madras on 20th December 1850. He came to Neyyoor and served as an active agent of the Gospel. His first wife died in Neyyoor on 25th February 1864 and married Anna Martha Cox on 25th February 1864. He was pioneer in implementing the new administrative system in the churches in South Travancore. In 1860 the native evangelists Esuvadian was promoted as a Deputy Head missionary to South Travancore. He started the Tamil magazine '*Desaupakari*' and he continued this work from 1861 to 1877. In 1864, workers class and scripture examinations were introduced for the first time to elevate Bible knowledge of the native church workers. In 1867, he appointed deacons to the church. He endeavored to make the church to move forward as a self supporting church and in 1863 the Nagercoil Church (now it is called as Home Church) achieved this status. On 13th February 1866 four of the native evangelists, Esuvadian, N. Devadason, S. Zahariah and Masilamoni were ordained to priesthood at Nagercoil. After the death of Baylis in Muttom on 17th May 1877, his wife was appointed as agent of the female mission of the society at Neyyoor from 26th November 1877. On 26th September 1878, she married Thompson and after his death she was re-appointed to the female mission at Neyyoor (John A. Jacob, *Triple Jubilee Commemoration Volume,* 72-77).

116 John, Owen White House, *Register of Missionaries Deputations*, 168.

117 Leitch Charles (1861 to 1864) born on 31st, October 1822 at Edinburgh, studied at the United Presbyterian Hall and Theological Academy, Glasgow. He obtained his degree in medicine from Edinburgh. He was ordained on 4th September 1851 at Greyfriars Church, Glasgow. On 1st July 1854, Mr. Baylis who came from Madras went to the sea at Muttom for bathing. He was drowned while bathing on 25th August 1854. He was a medical missionary from Scotland to South Travancore. He was sent by the Mission Society to India on 16th September 1851 and arrived at Madras on 17th December 1851. He remained in Madras until May 1852, studied forms of Indian disease in the hospitals and dispensaries in the city. From 15th February 1863, he went and resided in Neyyoor and was solely in charge of the Mission. On 7th March 1853, he opened a dispensary at Neyyoor which later it became a hospital. He made the entry to Nagercoil on 21st June 1852. He went and stayed in Santhapuram, one of the mission centers functioning under Neyyoor Mission district until February, 1853 (John A. Jacob, *Triple Jubilee Commemoration*

the responsibility to look after both the medical and mission work in Neyyoor mission district.[118] The arrival of the physician Rev. Leitch in 1861 brought new hope to the health care work in South Travancore. In a short period he started a Dispensary at Neyyoor, as the first Hospital in the whole of South Travancore. Lowe started the Medical Class in the Neyyoor centre to train the native assistants to be employed in the Branches as Medical Evangelists. In November 1864 a class commenced the study of medicine and surgery and to train a few native young men as medical assistants or dressers. From each Mission District young people, well educated in English, was selected and sent to Neyyoor for medical training. They were carefully instructed and trained for three years.[119]

James Duthie (1856 to 1891) was appointed and sent by the Mission Society on 4th February 1856 to South Travancore. He was born on 22nd September 1823 at Stonehaven and was ordained on 30th January 1856 at Bunyan Meeting, Bedford. In 1859 he took charge of the Seminary from J.W. Dennison and worked hard to start a college in South Travancore region to give higher education for the people living Travancore irrespective of caste and creed.[120] The upper cloth revolt came to an end in 1859. The missionaries' involvements in the upper cloth revolt for the oppressed strengthened the mission work in South Travancore the lower caste women were not allowed to wear upper cloths. But some of the Nadar women of South Travancore started to put on an additional piece of cloth across the breast and over one shoulder. The Nairs strongly objected to this practice because the upper cloth was traditional dress of their women. In May, 1822, Nadar women were ill treated for appearing in the market places with upper cloths. In the history of South Travancore, there were three protests against the attitude of Nair community towards the Nadar women. The protest for this human

---

Volume, 64, John Owen White House, *Register of Missionaries Deputations* 172).

118 John A. Jacob, *Triple Jubilee Commemoration Volume,* 64.

119 Samuel Mateer, *The Land of Charity*, The Living Stone Press, London, 1870, 312.

120 I. H. Hacker, *Register of Missionaries Deputations*, 51.

right was recorded in history as Upper Cloth Revolt. The revolts took place in the year 1882, 1828-29&1858 in different parts of South Travancore. The Nadar community was victimized and the court was in favour of Nairs. The missionaries of LMS especially, missionaries Charles Mead and John Cox stood against the injustice caused by the high caste people. Because of their continuous struggle and protest, a new proclamation was issued by the Madras Government on 26th July, 1859[121] which announced that,

> "There is no objection to Shanar women either putting on a jacket like the Christian Shanar women, or to Shanar women of all creeds dressing in coarsecloth(Kattisila) and tying themselves round with it as the Mukkvathikals (the low caste fisher women) do, or to their covering their bosoms in any manners whatever, but not like the women of high caste."[122]

The missionaries also served for short time in different mission station of South Travancore. [123]

In 1860 the Travancore District Committee (TDC) was formed for the smooth functioning of the churches. The mission understood the need for Indian leadership. The mission came forward to ordain eight Indians on 13th February 1866, working as an evangelist in different mission fields. To share the responsibilities and develop leadership qualities the new pastorate were formed in both Neyyoor and Nagercoil mission districts in 1879.[124] In the year 1866 the mission had 135 churches in Nagercoil, James Town, Santhapuram, Tittuvilai and Neyyoor.[125] On 28th July 1874, the South Travancore Church Council was formed and the Council had its first meeting

---

121 J.W. Gladstone, 19th Century Mass Movement in South Travancore- A Result of Social Liberation, ICHR, Vol. X, No: 1, Bangalore, 1976, p. 62 & 63.

122 Directorate of State Archives, Proclamation from 1858-1874, (Malayalam) Document No: 9, Trivandrum.

123 Missionaries served for short time- Lee William (1865-1884) Mabbs Goodeve (1865-1867), Nagercoil mission district. James Frank Gannaway (1861-1864) and Lowe John (1861-1868) served as a medical missionaries in Neyyoor.

124 John A. Jacob, *Triple Jubilee Commemoration Volume,* 80.

125 I. H. Hacker, *A Hundred Years in Travancore,* 56.

at Neyyoor. This was an advisory board to create an organization called 'The Union of Travancore Churches.' The native workers and congregation members from each district were given the place to serve as an ex-officio in South Travancore Church Council. The body made resolutions on self–support, social regulations, and on similar subjects and send it for the approval of Travancore District Committee.[126] During this period there was an expansion of mission work in church planting, establishment of schools and the opening of new health care units.

3.4. Mission Growth towards Union (1890 to 1947)

Rev. James Dathie (1856 to 1891), Rev. I.H. Hacker (1878 to 1920), Rev. Robert Sinclair (1909 to 1939), were the leading missionaries of this period served in different parts of south Travancore and established churches and also worked hard to the total development of the mission schools and other projects that were functioning in different mission stations.[127] During this period special missionaries were sent by the mission board to look after health care and education. J.W. Dennison (1892 to 1898), George Parker (1900 to 1927), Sydney Cave (1909 to 1916), Rev. R.H. Eastaff (1920 to 1950) and Rev. G.H. Marsden (1927 to 1957), were the missionaries served as a professors and principals of the newly established Scott Christian College in South Travancore. Miss. M.E. Mac Donnel (1891 to 1911), Dr. Davidson (1905 to 1914), Dr. T. Somervell (1923 to 1945), Dr. Ian M Orr (1927 to 1936) and Miss. Dr. John Thompson (1936 to 1950) came to South Travancore and served as the medical missionaries and also contributed to the development of health care by opening new healthcare units in different mission station of LMS in South Travancore.[128]

In the beginning of the 20th century there were 140 village schools and 20 girl schools, a college, and hospital was functioning in South Travancore. The following missionaries were sent by the

126 John A. Jacob, *A History of the London Missionary Society in Travancore,* 158.

127 Dr. Prabavathi Thayalan, Dr. Jeyasingh and Prof. Rajayadhas, *Pioneer Missionaries of Marthandam and Parasalai* (Tamil), Tower Grafics Printers, Nagercoil, 2000, 101.

128 G. Christdhas, *Paathachuvadukal*, 281ff.

Mission Board to give leadership in church planting, establish schools and hospitals in the mission fields of LMS in Nagercoil and Neyyoor mission districts.[129] In the year 1918 there were 24 churches functioning as pastorates in and around Nagercoil, Thittuvilai, Kottaram. James Town. Santhapuram, Neyyoor and Marthandam mission fields. The south Travancore Church Union was formed on 27th February 1904. James Duthie was the chairperson and the purpose of this union was to strengthen the pastorates and to elevate to the level of self supporting pastorates.[130] In 1906, the mission had its Centenary celebrations for three days from December 22 to 25 and representatives from 15 missionary societies were represented in the meeting.[131] The health care mission started in the year 1838 by Ramsay, developed as a main hospital in Neyyoor with six branch hospitals in south Travancore.[132]

In the year 1905 the missions in south Travancore, Madurai and Jaffna united under the leadership of James Dathie and formed "The South India United Church" on 25th July 1908 (SIUC). The purpose of SIUC was to bring unity and harmony among the missionaries and the mission body working in different parts of South India.[133] In 1920 Travancore Church Council (TCC) was formed to look after the administration of mission schools, lands, and hospital. The first council was held in Nagercoil and delegates from Pastorate and non-pastorate churches were represented together with the missionaries in decision making.[134] From the year 1932 the Travancore Church Council recognizes the Indian leadership and Rev. J.M. Kesari an Indian pastor was promoted as the District minister to the Neyyoor mission station.[135] In 1945 LMS had its 150th year celebration from 21st to 23rd September. Rev. Legg chaired the celebrations and

---

129 Dr. S.S Hector, *Then Thiruvithankooril Protestanat Missionkalin Samuthaya Vallarchiahal,* 156.

130 John A. Jacob, *A History of the London Missionary Society in Travancore,* 194.

131 John A. Jacob, *A History of the London Missionary Society in Travancore,* 187.

132 John A. Jacob, *A History of the London Missionary Society in Travancore,* 188.

133 G. Christdhas, *Paathachuvadukal,* 226.

134 John A. Jacob, *A History of the London Missionary Society in Travancore,* 212.

135 John A. Jacob, *A History of the London Missionary Society in Travancore,* 212.

Dewan C.P. Ramaswamy was the chief guest for the celebration.[136] Nationalism became deeply rooted among the people because of the educational activities of the LMS missionaries in South Travancore. Marshal Nesamony a senior lawyer was prepared to give political leadership. This awareness reflected in the churches and people were willing to have the leadership in the church committees at various level. It was in this period the Travancore Cochin Government passed the Compulsory Education Scheme in 1946 and many of the mission schools were surrendered to the Government for twelve years lease.[137]

The Travancore Church Council and the Mission Council came to the understanding with different Mission Bodies working in various places in south India. To avoid disputes in the working areas and also to strengthen the mission work the missionaries felt the need for having the union of churches. In 1947 the numbers of the churches were increased to 224 and the work was expanded with four mission districts (Nagercoil, Kottaram, James Town, Neyyoor, Marthandam, Santhapuram).[138] The church union was approved by church council and the Board of Directors of LMS at the first meeting in January 1948. Then, after 141 years (1806 to 1947) the mission formed South Travancore Diocese and joint with the Church of South India on 13th October 1947 and continued its work under the leadership of Bishop A.H. Legg who was a missionary served in Trivandrum Mission district from 1924.[139]

Conclusion

The arrival of the LMS missionaries brought forth changes in the spiritual, social and economic life of the native people especially among the so-called low caste people in south Travancore. Establishment of mission centers and the formation of Churches, schools, and other Institutions came to be a testimony to the vast changes that came in the life of the uncared sections of the region.

136 Desaupakari, LMS's Monthly Magazine, LMS Press, Nagercoil, 1945, p. 15.

137 Primary Education Act No. V111, M.E. 1121, Travancore Government, 1946.

138 John A. Jacob, *A History of the London Missionary Society in Travancore,* 187.

139 G. Christdhas, *Paathachuvadukal,* 235.

Education, once the monopoly of the high castes, now came to the villages of the underprivileged to make the same common affair. Administrative system was brought in by the missionaries to improve the strength and unity of the Church. To strengthen the growth and the unity of the church the South Travancore Church Council and new pastorate were formed to impart and develop a self-supporting ministry. To bring creative local leadership in the established churches and institutions, a catechist's theological class was started at Nagercoil. As a result of the mission work, the people were able to come out and react to the stigma of bondage and oppression imposed by 'the high castes'. The progressive activities of missionaries created self-confidence among the so-called low caste people who were suffering under the dehumanizing systems of the society. The approach of the missionaries towards social injustice and inequality, and their continuous efforts to bring people from the status of degradation to better humanhood brought radical changes in the life of the people. It gave impetus to the people to stand along with the missionaries to improve their social condition. Their reforming activities challenged the oppressive tendencies that were religiously sanctioned and historically perpetuated. In order to stand for the cause of the people, the missionaries fought with the government to bring the necessary legal amendments to protect the rights of the so-called lower castes.

The straightforward endeavor of the missionaries helped the interests of the low caste people to be restored and protected. As part of their mission focus, the missionaries contributed much to the education of the native people by establishing schools and a college. They introduced employment schemes like tailoring and lace making, and encouraged women's education. Health Care Mission was given much importance by the LMS Missionaries. They attempted to bring development in all aspects of life of the native people. In the area of health-care and education their contributions were commendable. It is an undeniable fact that the missionary contributions gave the converts Christians a better status in society, where the caste oppression prevailed. Even though the Mission Society had different thrusts and methods, its main focus was the liberation of people who were under extreme marginalization. It is also to be noted that comparing to other missionary groups, the work of the LMS was multi-faceted. The English missionaries came to South Travancore in the early 19th century were able to extend their territory within a short period, particularly the mission of LMS and its progressiveness was remarkable. The following chapters give the narration of detailed work of the LMS and its various features of Health Care and Education from 1890 to 1947 in South Travancore.

Chapter 3

Health Care Mission in South Travancore (1890 to 1947)

Introduction

In the beginning of the 19th century, western medical facilities and modes of treatments were totally absent in South Travancore. The people were fully depended upon the native medical men who used to charge heavily for medical treatment. Therefore in most of the cases, patients would go to a physician only at a critical stage. The native medical facility was not only unaffordable but also inaccessible to the low caste people. The more respectable type of native treatment was Ayurvedic. The Ayurvedic treatment was done mainly based on the nature of symptoms. But the native medical methods were not much successful to prevent the dangerous diseases of the people. At the same time, many died due to the lack of proper medical treatment. In this situation, the LMS medical missionaries who recognized the value of life started their health care mission to save the people. The medical missionaries started to come from the year 1838 and involved fully in different types of health care activities. In order to provide the proper medical treatment to the in and out patients, they offered western medicine in the mission clinics and hospitals. During the period of 1890 to 1947, LMS health care mission brought many positive changes in their approach to health care mission. Because of the committed life of LMS health care medical missionaries the health care mission became much effective in South Travancore. Hence, this chapter deals with the contributions of LMS on Health Care service from the year 1890-1947.

1. The Beginning of Health Care Mission

One of the areas in which the Christian missionaries contributed a lot in India, in spite of their small size and economic disabilities, is Health Care. The LMS started its mission work at Mylaudy in 1806. Charles Mead developed the idea of introducing the Health Care Mission in south Travancore. In London, Mead met the trained Doctor Archibald Ramsay and requested Home Board to send Ramsay to South Travancore to start the proposed Health Care Mission in 1838. He was the second Medical[1] Missionary sent forth by the LMS and the first to South Travancore.[2] During the Palmyra season, the poor Palmyra climbers frequently met with accidents of a very serious nature. The untouchable diseases like leprosy and cancer were common and people were left without care and not considered as part of the society. The condition of women and children was far from satisfactory. Large number of children died immediately after birth due to the deficiency of proper child care measures. The condition of pregnant women was worse than any one else's. Even in the houses they were attended by the village midwife who was an illiterate, untrained and was hygienic midwife. In the beginning of the 19th century People of this region were on the opinion that evil spirits as the cause of their disease. Health care mission not only acted as an auxiliary to accelerate the propagation of the faith but also an agency to efface the social evils of various other dimensions.[3]

1 The Society's first Medical Missionary was Dr. John Taylor appointed for Surat in 1804.

2 N. Martin Daniel Dhas, *Missionary Medical Work in Travancore, 1838-1958*, 13.

3 Samuel Mateer, *The Land of Charity*, John Snow and Company, London, 1871, 284.

The health care mission gave the idea to the people that the medicine had healing powers against these evil spirits.[4]

The dispensary in South Travancore was established by Dr. Charles Leitch and in 1861 the hospital became a self-sufficient unit.[5] In 1861 Dr. John Lowe was sent to south Travancore and there was a substantial increase in medical work after his arrival.[6] The Maharaja recognized his work to his people and hence gave an annual grant for its support.[7] Famine followed by diseases occurred frequently and 1880 people suffered under great starvation. Small-pox and Cholera infected the people regularly.[8] Then its ravages carried off thousands in a very short space of time.[9] In 1888 a great epidemic of Cholera swept over the life of about 2000 Christians close to Neyyoor Mission District.[10] The Government was absolutely helpless to do things to the advantage of the affected.[11] Under the said state of affairs and circumstances the LMS in South Travancore thought of introducing Health Care Mission as a viable auxiliary for the propagation of the faith. The LMS missionaries contributed to health care work in the above said period to save the life of the people in South Travancore.

2. Progress of Health Care Mission (1890 to 1947)

The LMS medical missionaries came in different period contributed much to the health care mission and they were able to save the life of the people from epidemics incurable diseases. Dr. John Lowe

---

4 T. Howard Somervell, *Knife and Life in India: The Story of a Surgical Missionary at Neyyoor,* 93.

5 N. Martin Daniel Dhas, *Missionary Medical Work in Travancore, 1838-1958,* 26.

6 John Suresh Kumar, Christian Medical Care in Tamil Nadu, Vol. XXXV11/ 2, December, 2003, Indian *Church History Review*, Church History Association of India, Banglore, 102.

7 I.H. Hacker, *A Hundred Years in South Travancore*, 57.

8 Annual Report of the South Travancore Mission Hospital and Dispensaries for the year 1880, 5.

9 Report of the Santhapuram Mission District for the year 1860, 2.

10 I.H. Hacker, *A Hundred Years in South Travancore*, 59.

11 Annual Report of the Neyyoor Mission District, 1860, 5.

tried to send his son-in- law, Dr. Edwin Sargood Fry,[12] M.B.C.M. to Travancore.[13] In 1889 Dr. Fry started medical classes. Mrs. Fry also helped the medical students.[14] After the death of Dr. Edwin Sargood Fry the LMS sent Dr. Arthur Fells [15] to take over the South

12 Dr. Edwin Sargood Fry (*1886- 1892),* was born on 27th November 1858 at Chemford. He did his Medical education in Edinbarow Medical College. He began his voyage for India on 23rd December 1885. Dr. and Mrs. Sargood Fry reached Neyyoor on 11th February 1886. Mrs. Fry was born in Neyyoor itself twenty years back when her father Dr. John Lowe was a Doctor. He was the family Doctor of the late Dewan Nanoo Pillai. After the death of Dr. Thomson, the South Travancore Medical Mission once again became one without a Missionary Doctor for two years. During this period the Neyyoor Evangelical Missionary H. Hacker supervised the Medical Mission. Hospital work was mainly looked after by Dr. R.P. Packianathan, Chief Medical Evangelist of the Neyyoor Hospital. Apart from his medical work, he involved in evangelistic activities. Every Sunday Dr. Fry went to Eraniel to preach the Gospel among the Hindus. Once in a month he went to Padmanabhapuram to preach the Word of God among the non-Christians. He translated twelve sermons into Tamil in 1892. His continuous strain greatly affected his health and he fell ill and died on 20th December 1892 at the age of 56 (N. Martin Daniel Dhas, *Missionary Medical Work in Travancore, 1838-1958,* 15, 16).

13 N. Martin Daniel Dhas, *Missionary Medical Work in Travancore, 1838-1958,* 14.

14 Samuel Zechariah, *A Summery of the History of the Church in South Travancore, 1855-1906* (Tamil), Part 11, LMS Press, Nagercoil, 1906, 144ff.

15 Dr. Arthur Fells (1893-1905), on 31st December 1862 sailed the vessel R.M.S. Ophir with his wife and reached Colachel on 30th January 1893. The other Missionaries of the place and the native Christians welcomed the Fells couple with great Joy. After working for nearly seven years in Travancore, Dr. Fells thought of to have an unpaid leave. So he asked the Board at Home to send another Medical Missionary during his absence. Accordingly, S.H. Davies was appointed temporarily to Travancore. He arrived at Neyyoor on 31st January 1901. Dr. Fells took furlough. In November Dr. Fell returned to Neyyoor from furlough at the end of 1901 and in December Dr. Davies left Travancore. In 1905 Dr. Fells resigned and left the Medical Mission on account of his family circumstances. As his co-worker Dr. Bentall wrote, the annual number of patients went up from 26,000 to 70,000 and the expenditure from Rs. 6,000 to 20,000 while the branches increased from seven to thirteen. These are mere figures which we all recognize and are not complete indication of the progress and condition of that side of the work which we put first. His successor Bental says, Fells was an ideal Medical Missionary. He practiced what he preached

Travancore Health Care Mission.[16] The first effort of Fells was to finish teaching the medical students at the stage where it was left by Dr. Fry.[17] He opened the way for starting Medical work in new places and the old station also Agusteespuram was re-opened.[18] LMS appointed William Charles Bentall[19] to South Travancore.[20] Dr. Bentall took delight to travel over the District and preferred to cycle often ten to fourteen miles an hour.[21] With the generosity of his friends in New Castle, he could build two new clean wards.[22] In April 1906 Dr. Bentall made an extensive tour through various districts, visiting Branch Hospitals and Dispensaries.[23]

Dr. James Davidson came to Neyyoor in 1905 and worked in the medical mission till 1913.[24] His period saw the erection of a separate Eye Ward in the Central Hospital at Neyyoor.[25] He started

---

and his life made an indelible impression on the higher class Hindus." He was the First Surgeon in the whole of India. (Samuel Zechariah, *A Summery of the History of the Church in South Travancore, 1855-1906, Part II*, 158; Annual Report of the South Travancore L.M.S. Medical Mission, 1900, 14; Martin Daniel Dhas, *Missionary Medical Work in Travancore, 1838-1958*, 52f).

16 N. Martin Daniel Dhas, *Missionary Medical Work in Travancore, 1838-1958*, 49.

17 Samuel Zechariah, *A Summery of the History of the Church in South Travancore*, (Tamil), Part 11, 159.

18 Annual Report of the L.M.S. Medical Mission, 1900, 4.

19 Dr. Bentall (1902-1907), arrived at Nagercoil in January 1902 and began to learn Tamil. In 1904 a new building for the Mission Dispensary at Nagercoil was opened. In 1907 he resigned due to ill health of his wife and returned to England. His Missionary experience in Travancore exerted a powerful influence on the Home Board, which took him once as a Director of the Board and then as its Chairman (N. Martin Daniel Dhas, *Missionary Medical Work in Travancore, 1838-1958,* 51f).

20 N. Martin Daniel Dhas, *Missionary Medical Work in Travancore, 1838-1958,* 51.

21 Report of the Ten years work in connection with South Travancore Medical Mission, 1901-1910, 14.

22 Report of the South Travancore Medical Mission, 1909, 6.

23 Annual Report of the South Travancore Medical Mission, 1906, 12.

24 N. Martin Daniel Dhas, *Missionary Medical Work in Travancore, 1838-1958*, 55ff.

25 Annual Report of the South Travancore Medical Mission, 1910, 13.

the compounder's class at Neyyoor and taught the medical Students the subjects of Anatomy and 'Meteria Medica'.[26] He helped the poor with money or other gifts.[27] In February two small private wards were added to the central hospital and in March 1913 he went home on unpaid leave.[28] In February 1913, Dr. O. H. Bulloch[29] arrived from England to South Travancore and was able to serve in Medical Mission only for two years.[30] Dr. Bulloch took some ward clinics, supervised the work of the students in their ward Clinics, as well as the work of the students in their ward dressings. In the New Year he gave lecture on Public Health and Health Care.[31]

In the place of Dr. James Davidson the Home Board sent Dr. S.H. Pugh[32] and he came to Neyyoor in 1913 and continued his health care work till 1948. He increased the efficiency and size of the Hospital tremendously.[33] Dr. Pugh encouraged and helped the men trained in the American Presbyterian Mission Medical School at Bombay. The entire cost of education of those candidates was met

---

26 Report of the South Travancore Medical Mission, 1911, 11.

27 Annual Report of the South Travancore Medical Mission, 1908, 18.

28 Report of the Ten years work in connection with the South Travancore Medical Mission, 1913, 8.

29 Dr. O. H. Bulloch arrived from England to take Dr. Orrin's place. The extreme hot climate of the time forced him to retire to the Hills. Dr. Bulloch taught the Medical Students the subject of Physiology. He visited Branch Hospitals by cycling during every Sunday. He married the daughter of Dr. Pugh who came to Neyyoor in 1912. In 1913 his wife fell ill and at the beginning of November Dr. Bulloch was obliged to leave Neyyoor and went to England. (Report of the South Travancore Medical Mission, 1911, 8ff).

30 Report of the South Travancore Medical Mission, 1911, 8.

31 Annual Report of the South Travancore Medical Mission, 1913, 10-19.

32 Dr. Stephen Horatio Pugh, M.B.Ch., B.F.R.C.S., came to the South Travancore Medical Mission in 1913. Dr. Pugh was very tired of over work and was therefore recommended for leave. Dr. S.H. Pugh died of heart failure on 19th August 1948 after an illness of several weeks. (N. Martin Daniel Dhas, *Missionary Medical Work in Travancore, 1838-1958*, 57, 61 and LMS Report of the Institutional work Industries and properties under the supervision of the Mission council, 1926, 13.

33 Annual Report of the South Travancore Medical Mission, 1926, 12.

by the Health Mission.[34] During his time Dr. Somervell visited the Neyyoor Hospital in September 1922. The two doctors together performed a number of Surgical Operations.[35] Dr. Pugh's untiring efforts enabled the hospital to fill the eighty beds and to keep the wards full in the year 1926.[36] Dr. A. P. Thomas[37] came to South Travancore and took charge of the Health Mission from Dr. Bullock in December 1913,[38] Dr. Orr[39] served in the Health Mission and was helpful to D. Somervell in the Mission hospital at Neyyoor. From

34 N. Martin Daniel Dhas, *Missionary Medical Work in Travancore, 1838-1958*, 58.

35 N. Martin Daniel Dhas. *Missionary Medical Work in Travancore, 1838-1958*, 60.

36 N. Martin Daniel Dhas., *Missionary Medical Work in Travancore, 1838-1958*, 61.

37 Mrs. A. P. Thomas was a daughter of Dr. E. Sargood Fry who was a former Medical Missionary in Neyyoor. The people of Neyyoor gave a hearty welcome to Dr. and Mrs. A. P. Thomas (1913-1916), During September and October he and his wife had a most interesting and encouraging tour around the Northern Branches. They spent from three to eight days in each Hospital. He preached Gospel every day. In 1916 he was recalled by the Society. So he and his wife returned home in February to be engaged in war service. He worked hard in a Military Hospital in England. (Annual Meeting of the South Travancore Diocesan Council, 1948, 13 and Annual Report of the South Travancore Medical Mission, 1926, 9).

38 Annual Meeting of the South Travancore Diocesan Council, 1948, CSI, Diocesan Office, 13.

39 Dr. Orr arrived from furlough at the end of September. He spent most of his spare time for research on Cancer. The Indian Medical Staff at Neyyoor did their share of the work, enabling Dr. Orr to find time for research on the cause and treatment of the duodenal ulcer, the most important disease. Dr. Orr was a first-class Surgeon and he worked with Dr. Somervell in the surgical section. He was called by Miraj Medical School and he left Neyyoor in 1937 to accept an appointment at the Miraj Medical School. There he worked efficiently for nine years continuously. After a long and fruitful service in the Medical Mission, this great Missionary Doctor officially retired from it in 1945. Surprisingly, Dr. Somervell again came to Neyyoor in 1948 and took over the Medical Mission as its Medical Superintendent and as the Chairman of the Medical Board. (Travancore Mission Council Reports and Accounts for the academic year 1993 – 34,36, Report of the South Travancore Medical Mission, 1932, 5, LMS Travancore Mission Council Reports and Accounts,

18th January 1914 Dr. A.P. Thomas began to take care of the diseases of children.[40] He maintained the activities of the Health Mission during four terrible year of war.[41]

These medical missionaries contributed to the general development for the health care mission in South Travancore. They involved in several scope of works, such as begging of an eye ward, opening of health care units, constructing new wards to accommodate and treat the inpatients, encouraging the native people to involve in nursing care and giving them health care education, and the concern for health care to children. Because of their commitment and hard work the mission was able to make an impact among the people and also they were well established and recognized in Neyyoor.

3. Impact of Health Care Mission

3.1. Health Care for Women

The other notable development and impact of LMS service was on the area of health care for women, health care for lepers, and health care for cancer patients of the people in South Travancore. Miss. Margaret MacDonnell who was appointed in 1892 at the time of Dr. Fry, continued her service till 1911. She was the first lady Nursing Superintendent and also the first qualified staff nurse to be sent by LMS as medical missionary to South Travancore. The nursing care was very much associated with the name of MacDonnell. She began to train nurses in the Neyyoor Hospital for the first time.[42] She was the pioneer in maternity work. It was due to her zeal in raising funds as well as in training helpers that the first maternity ward was built at Neyyoor.[43] Miss. MacDonnell and Dr. Fells worked together and a

---

1936, 5, L.M.S. Ten years Church and Mission in Travancore, 1931-40, 2, N. Martin Daniel Dhas, *Missionary Medical Work in Travancore, 1838-1958,* 65).

40 Annual Report of the South Travancore Medical Mission, 1926, 9.

41 Annual Report of the South Travancore Medical Mission, 1926, 8.

42 Annual Report of the South Travancore Medical Mission, 1900, 4.

43 Norman Goodall, *A History of the London Missionary Society, 1895-1945,* London: Oxford University Press, 1954, 51.

separate Maternity Ward was built at a cost of Rs.4,000/-[44] And also she was an instrumental in starting a medical shop at Nagercoil.[45] Dr. Pugh served single handedly in all his work and this was devotedly supported by his wife, who looked after all the orphans and the women's Leper Home.[46] Mrs. Charles Peace donated Rs.1,739/- for the female leper home through the Mission.[47] Dr. Fell built a separate home for the women Lepers in Neyyoor with the gift of Mrs. Charles Peace and opened the new home on New Year's Day of 1901.[48]

Edith Hacker served with the mission from 1923 to 1927. She was the daughter of a missionary and she brought reform in nursing care. In her period the number of missionary nurses was increased. Missionaries, namely Eileen Pidcock, Edith Mills (1926), Gwyneth Lawrence (1928) arrived at South Travancore and served as missionary nurses in Neyyoor Mission Hospitals.[49] Dr. Theodore Howard Somervell[50] thought of joining South Travancore Health Mission to become its second Surgeon when Miss. Hacker was the

---

44 N. Martin Daniel Dhas, *Missionary Medical Work in Travancore, 1838-1958*, 50.

45 Annual Report of the South Travancore L.M.S. Medical Mission, 1897, 7.

46 Annual Report of the South Travancore Medical Mission, 1926, 14.

47 Martin Daniel Dhas, *Missionary Medical Work in Travancore, 1838-1958*, 50.

48 N. Martin Daniel Dhas, *Missionary Medical Work in Travancore, 1838-1958*, 141.

49 Norman Goodall, *A History of the London Missionary Society, 1895-1945*, 51.

50 Theodore Howard Somervell (1924-*1949*), M.A., M.B.B.Ch., F.R.C.S. was born in Kendal, in the United Kingdom in 1880. His father W. H. Somervell was a honorary Treasurer of the L.M.S. from 1918 till 1930. Dr. Somervell was a very good mountaineer and came to India in 1924 for Everest Expedition. As he had heard about the L.M.S. in Travancore and its Medical Centre at Neyyoor, he came to Neyyoor from Himalayas to see the place. There at Neyyoor he was surprised by Dr. Pugh's service in Travancore. In 1949 he went to Vellore. However, he came back and worked again at Neyyoor during 1950-51. Dr. Somervell again came to Neyyoor in 1948 and took over the Medical Mission as its Medical Superintendent and as the Chairman of the Medical Board. He went back to Vellore during 1951-1953. Finally he retired from Missionary work in 1954 and returned to England to spend his last days (N. Martin Daniel Dhas, *Missionary Medical Work in Travancore, 1838-1958* 65, 79, Annual Reports of the South Travancore Medical Mission 1992,10 and 1918, 9).

Nursing Superintendent.[51] As soon as he assumed charge of the Health Mission, the Hospital was more crowded than ever before. Additional wards were built to provide forty four more beds. A separate ward for women patients was also built in the Hospital Compound. In 1925 it is estimated that 1,20,059 patients were treated and 188 major and 5,309 minor operations were performed.[52] Dr. Joan Thompson came in 1936 and she rendered her service to health care mission till 1950. She was the first qualified Missionary Woman Doctor of the South Travancore Health Mission. After her arrival, the number of women patients increased considerably.[53] She studied Tamil language and began her work at Neyyoor.[54] She trained women in midwifery and two of them were Devai and Paripuranan.[55] During this period women missionary doctors namely Dr. James (1942-1946), Dr. R. Allani (1946-1947), and concentrated particularly on women health care in South Travancore.[56] Dr. Fell built a separate home for the women Lepers in Neyyoor with the gift of Mrs. Charles Pease.[57]

3.2. Health Care for Cancer Patients

Dr. T.H. Somerwell constructed a radium ward for the treatment of cancer disease which was started in 1931. He wanted to treat cancer with Radium.[58] He used radium needless and introduced the new method of Heminandibletomy Operation for the cancer disease.[59] For giving the treatment to the Cancer patients he purchased Rs. 1000/- worth of Radium. In 1931 he opened the 'Radium Wards' in the Central Hospital. They were inaugurated by Col. Pritchard,

---

51 N. Martin Daniel Dhas, *Missionary Medical Work in Travancore, 1838-1958*, 65.

52 The Hundred and Thirtieth Report of the LMS, 1925, 29.

53 L.M.S. Travancore Mission Council Reports and Accounts, 1939, 36.

54 L.M.S. Travancore Mission Council Reports and Accounts, 193, 36.

55 J.R. Hepzi Joy, *History and Development of Education of Women in Kerala*, 98.

56 L.M.S. Travancore Mission Council Reports and Accounts, 1939, 37.

57 N. Martin Daniel Dhas, *Missionary Medical Work in Travancore, 1838-1958*, 141.

58 Report of the South Travancore Medical Mission, 1930, 5.

59 Dr. Selin Joyal, Cancer Patients, *Desaupakari*, CSI Kanyakumari Diocese, February, 2008, 13.

the Agent to the Governor General.[60] Somervell took special care to give free medicine and food to the poorest patients.[61]

Fees were collected from the patients who were rich enough to meet the expenses for the treatment for both X-ray and surgery.[62] In 1938 South Travancore Health Mission completed its one hundred years of service. The LMS in Travancore celebrated the occasion by inaugurating a New Ward and an out-patient ward in the Central Hospital.[63] In 1945 this great Missionary Doctor officially retired from the Health Mission of Neyyoor. After him Dr. Fells took interest to publish an article on "Cancer of the Mouth in South India" with an analysis of 209 operations.[64] He has rightly been referred to as "the Ideal Health Care Missionary". He combined a remarkable degree of professional skill, both Health Care and Surgical, particularly in ophthalmic practice with a deeply religious and consistent life.[65] This cancer ward became the International Cancer Centre along with the Central Hospital at Neyyoor in 1963.[66]

---

60 Annual Report of the South Travancore LMS Medical Mission, 1931, 6.

61 Annual Report of the South Travancore LMS Medical Mission, 1931, 7.

62 Annual Report of the South Travancore Medical Mission, 1930, 5.

63 N. Martin Daniel Dhas, *Missionary Medical Work in Travancore, 1838-1958*, 75.

64 Report of the South Travancore Medical Mission, 1908, Kanyakumari Medical Mission Neyyoor, 24.

65 Report of the Ten years work in connection with the South Travancore Medical Mission, 1910, 11.

66 M. Gopalakrishnan (Ed), *Gazetteers of India, Tamilnadu State, Kanyakumari District,* Madras : Printers Industrial Co-operative Society, 1995, 1093.

3.3. Health Care for Lepers

Dr. Sargood Fry once met a leprosy[67] affected beggar. The poor leper followed the physician for about six miles begging for help.[68] The plight of this poor beggar touched the heart of the Missionary and there he decided to provide a leprosy ward in the General Hospital at Neyyoor.[69] In view of cherishing this desire he wrote to the Mission to Lepers in October 1887 seeking financial assistance. The Mission Board Committee's met on 24th November and passed an immediate grant for the erection of a ward.[70] The hospital was named after the donor's name as 'Charles Peace Memorial Leprosy Hospital'.[71] The aim of this Mission was "to alleviate the pressing symptoms, to minimize the spread of the disease among the healthy and to make known among those laden with crushing sorrow, the loving sympathy of the "Man of sorrows".[72] The next year of Dr. Fry's arrival at Neyyoor was marked by the Jubilee Celebrations of Queen Victoria's reign throughout Travancore as in the other parts of the British Empire. In connection with these celebrations the LMS in South Travancore decided to erect a Jubilee Hospital and a 'Leper asylum' in Neyyoor.[73] The important aspect of Dr. Fry's period was the beginning of work among lepers. He collected some donations and erected 'Leper Asylum' at Neyyoor (near Neyyoor Hospital) in

67 Leprosy was considered as a dreadful disease considering that there was no treatment and medicine to cure the disease. The dread of infection and the stigma attached to the disease made the affected as objects of horror. To help the others to know the presence of the lepers in the public places and keep away from them, the poor lepers had to shout the word "Unclean - Unclean". People considered leprosy as a mysterious disease. And also this disease created peculiar social and economical problems among the people.

68 Joy Gnanadasan, *A Forgotten History*, 141.

69 Joy Gnanadasan, *A Forgotten History*, 142.

70 D. Christdhas, *A Short History of the C.P. Memorial Leprosy Hospital, in Leprosy Hospital's Jubilee Souvenior, LMS Press, Nagercoil, 1940*, 140.

71 D. Christdhas, *A Short History of the C.P. Memorial Leprosy Hospital*, 140.

72 D. Christudhas, *A Short History of the C.P. Memorial Leprosy Hospital*, 95.

73 N. Martin Daniel Dhas, *Missionary Medical Work in Travancore, 1838-1958*, 15.

1890. Later it was developed into Charles Pease Memorial Leprosy Hospital, Colachel.[74]

The Health Mission started leprosy work in 1890 by admitting a few wandering lepers in an isolated ward of the Neyyoor Hospital.[75] It was an Asylum for the protection and care for a few helpless victims of the society.[76] To save them from this crisis and to reduce the burden of the affected parents, the Mission thought of establishing a home for such children. Accordingly in 1890 a separate home for the children of the lepers was opened at Neyyoor. P.J. Cornelius, one of the Health Care Evangelists trained at Neyyoor, was the first Doctor, to care for the leprosy patients from 1893 to 1917. To the development of this work the authorities wanted to establish an asylum in a some what isolated place.[77] The Mission found a new leper asylum at Allankottay, the northern part of Neyyoor.[78] The first block of building was completed and opened on 11th August 1892 with twenty patients.[79] In the beginning both the male and female patients were treated in the same house. However, in course of time, separate homes were required for both male and female patients. As a consequence, Male Asylum with forty beds and a Female Home with twelve beds, flourished in the same campus.[80] The strength of the asylum for both men and women patients increased to eighty under Dr. P.J. Cornelius (1893-1920). In its growing stage he died in 1920. He served for more than thirty years. After him the work was

74 N. Martin Daniel Dhas, *Missionary Medical Work in Travancore, 1838-1958*, 46.

75 N. Martin Daniel Dhas, *Missionary Medical Work in Travancore, 1838-1958*, 140.

76 N. Martin Daniel Dhas, *Missionary Medical Work in Travancore, 1838-1958*, 141.

77 N. Martin Daniel Dhas, *Missionary Medical Work in Travancore, 1838-1958*, 140.

78 Joy Gnanadasan, *A Forgotten History*, 87.

79 Annual Report of the L.M.S. Medical Mission, 1899, 9.

80 Report of the Ten years work in connection with the South Travancore Medical Mission, 1901-1910, 33.

taken up by Dr. G.M. Samuel and M.W. Samuel served as Health Care assistance.[81]

Devadasan[82] an evangelist had a remarkable influence on the Leprosy patients, both men and women. Leprosy which was considered incurable in those days gradually came to be treated curable to a certain extent.[83] In 1927 alone eight patients out of thirty who were getting treatment received complete cure. Six of them were discharged to their homes free of all symptoms.[84] However, there was pressure from the public to shift the Home to an isolated place.[85] The Mission to Lepers came forward to meet the cost of construction on account of shifting the asylum to a distant place. The new Leper Home[86] was built in Udayarvilai in 1933. This Health Care endeavor to lepers became a hope for many hopeless and also a source of assistance to the state administration. A Doctor's House and four wards were opened by Mr. Austin, the Dewan of Travancore in 1933.[87] Having rendered faithful service to the Leper Home for

---

81 N. Martin Daniel Dhas, *Missionary Medical Work in Travancore, 1838-1958*, 141.

82 The Evangelist Devadasan (1920-1940), a Nair convert was in-charge of the Homes. He was active in his management and administered the bodily and spiritual needs of the patients. The Government of India had also been induced to bear the expense of the new treatment which was going on in Neyyoor (South Travancore Medical Mission Annual Report, 1928, 17; Travancore LMS Medical Mission Annual Report, 1919, 15).

83 N. Martin Daniel Dhas, *Missionary Medical Work in Travancore, 1838-1958*, 142.

84 N. Martin Daniel Dhas, *Missionary Medical Work in Travancore, 1838-1958*, 142.

85 D. Christdhas, *A Short History of the C.P. Memorial Leprosy Hospital*, 2.

86 The new Leper Home is situated at Udayarvilai about 2½ miles from Neyyoor on the Monday market – Colachel. It was opened on 17th November 1933 and is now going on in full swing. In about 5½ acres of healthy dry ground with a sprinkling of shade-giving trees, the Mission built four 'Houses' with large open door ways and windows providing unlimited supply of fresh air to the inmates. In South India, especially in South Travancore, Leprosy was undoubtedly on the increase, although the Government was taking measures for an increase of relief work (South Travancore Medical Mission L.M.S. Annual Report, 1933, 12).

87 D. Christdhas, *A Short History of the C.P. Memorial Leprosy Hospital*, 95.

many years Dr. Devadason retired in 1940.[88] He was succeeded by Dr. K. Abraham as the Medical Officer in the Leprosy Hospital. He had gained the special study of the disease.[89] Following the death of Dr. Abraham in 1938, Dr. Visuvasam came from Dohnavur to take Dr. Abraham's place. He also showed a real interest in the welfare of the patients.

Dr. D. Christ has served as Medical Superintendent of the Leprosy Hospital from 1938 to 1948. In his time the patients who got complete cure were employed in the Mission.[90] A new women's block was opened in 1937 and the female Lepers were shifted from Neyyoor to the new site. A Children's ward was added on to the Hospital in 1940 and an out-patient clinic in 1948.[91] During this period Higher Government Officials, representatives of various Missions and Boards, Heads of various Charitable Institutions and other Philanthropists from both India and foreign countries often visited the Hospital.[92] During this period the uncared and wandering lepers not only got shelter in the Leper Home of the Mission but also treatment for the disease. Leprosy hitherto considered incurable and contagious came to be treated with medicines and injections and proved that leprosy was curable and those who recovered from the disease could also lead a normal life in the society as others with recognition and equality.

3.4. Health Care Units

The early Health Care Missionaries were all along thinking of extending the Health Mission. Dr. John Lowe's great desire was to open a Branch Dispensary in each Mission District of the LMS field in South Travancore. Accordingly he and the other missionaries started health care units in Tittuvilai, Kulasekaram, Marthandam, Nagercoil and Santhapuram, which were considered to be the important localities of the Mission fields of Nagercoil and Neyyoor Mission

88 Annual Report of the South Travancore Medical Mission, 1938,

89 N. Martin Daniel Dhas, *Missionary Medical Work in Travancore, 1838-1958*, 145.

90 N. Martin Daniel Dhas, *Missionary Medical Work in Travancore, 1838-1958*, 145.

91 N. Martin Daniel Dhas, *Missionary Medical Work in Travancore, 1838-1958*, 147.

92 N. Martin Daniel Dhas, *Missionary Medical Work in Travancore, 1838-1958*, 147.

Districts.[93] Obviously it is found that thousands of people every year came to realize the value of treatment by scientific methods.[94] Most of the Branch Hospitals were established in the 19th century.[95] A large amount of medical work was done at the outstation Dispensaries and Hospitals. These Branch Hospitals and Dispensaries greatly added to the influence of the Medical Mission.[96]

In Tittuvilai[97] the people could make use of this Mission Dispensary at times of necessity.[98] People in large numbers came to the Dispensary to get medicines for their ailments. Very soon it was converted into a hospital following the erection of a Ward for the accommodation of six in-patients.[99] It is interesting to know that the work of this branch was carried on in an old "Chattram" or Inn used for the high caste people. The pillars of the building are still found with figures of local deities, but the healing ministry of the LMS was carried on in the building.[100] In the beginning of the twentieth century Travancore was passing through a period of great transition in every field. In the field of medical service, a number of Government Hospitals were opened. A lot of private medical practitioners also set up their own Dispensaries in many towns.[101] For these reasons some

93 N. Martin Daniel Dhas, *Missionary Medical Work in Travancore, 1838-1958*, 122.

94 Annual Report of the South Travancore Medical Mission, 1880, 9.

95 Howard Somervell, T. Howard Somervell, *Knife and Life in India: The Story of a Surgical Missionary at Neyyoor, Travancore,* The Living Stone Press, London, 1955, 138.

96 The One Hundred and Eleventh Report of the LMS, 1906, 120.

97 Tittuvilai is situated five miles North of Nagercoil and is very near to the foot of the Hills. It is in Nanjinad near the eastern side of the Western Ghats. Most of the people of Tittuvilai were agricultural coolies. To the benefit of this poor working class of that place Dr. T.S. Thompson opened a Dispensary in 1879. Around this place were many thickly populated towns and villages.

98 Annual Report of the South Travancore Medical Mission Hospital and Dispensaries, 1880, 16.

99 Report of the Ten years work in connection with the South Travancore Medical Mission, 1901-1910, 21.

100 Report of the Ten years work in connection with the South Travancore Medical Mission, 1901-1910, 22.

101 N. Martin Daniel Dhas, *Missionary Medical Work in Travancore, 1838-1958*, 123.

of the Branch Hospitals of the South Travancore Medical Mission in the Tamil area had to be closed down. Health Care units functioning in different mission fields at Tittuvilai, Agustesvram and Kottaram were closed due to this reason.[102]

Dr. Thompson opened a Dispensary at Kulasekaram.[103] The Dispensary was originally started in an old salt store. It was excessively dark and gloomy and could not be kept clean. By no means was it suited for the purpose. However, for want of space for immediate occupation it was divided into four or five compartments.[104] Very soon the Mission wanted to construct new buildings. As its financial position stood in the way, it thought of seeking financial assistance from the willing local public.[105] Many people in the neighborhood expressed their willingness to help. Some indeed had already subscribed either in money or timber. Thus the chance for the completion of the work appeared bright for the mission.[106] At first, the number of patients that came to this Dispensary was not so encouraging. So it was stopped for a while and again re-opened in February 1901.

The Dispensary was first started at Marthandam[107] on 18th July 1883 in a temporary shed in the present vegetable market.

---

102 N. Martin Daniel Dhas, *Missionary Medical Work in Travancore, 1838-1958*, 123.

103 Kulasekaram is five miles North of Attoor at the foot of the Hills. This place was notorious for Malaria fever. In addition to this the construction of the famous Pechipparai Dam made the Dispensary an indispensable one in the place. Hundreds of coolies came from different areas to be employed in the construction work were badly needed medical help at times of accidents and affliction of Malaria fever as well as other diseases. People of the places in and around Kulasekaram were economically very poor and their chance to take treatment in the distant Hospitals was very remote. Taking all these into consideration Dr. Thompson opened a Dispensary at Kulasekaram in 1880.

104 Annual Report of the South Travancore Medical Mission, 1899, 10.

105 Annual Report of the South Travancore Medical Mission, 1899, 11.

106 Annual Report of the South Travancore Medical Mission, 1899. 14.

107 Marthandam emerged as a rising Mission Centre under the supervision of Rev. James Emyln. It was this Missionary Emlyn who was responsible for the formation of the Pacode, Attoor and Viricode Roads from Marthandam. He was also mainly responsible for the establishment of a Market, Post and

Vethamanickam, a Medical Evangelist trained by Dr. T. S. Thompson was the first Physician to commence the work at Marthandam. Within a very short period it was shifted to the present location.[108] The Mission constructed a Maternity Ward and appointed a Nurse in that Station.[109] The people of the neighborhood could understand the Marthandam Hospital's close association with the big Hospital at Neyyoor. So they had the great advantage of taking very serious cases and patients requiring special advice to the Neyyoor Central Hospital.[110] Four Private Wards were opened and the cost of construction was completely given by Rev. R. Sinclair from Marthandam Embroidery Industry. The hospital was always over crowded with patients. This was largely due to the enthusiastic work of S.G. Manuel, the Medical Evangelist in-charge.[111]

Dr. T.S. Thomson opened the branch Dispensary at Santhapuram in 1876[112] which was a small but very neat Dispensary with four beds. For emergencies or special cases patients were given beds. The Dispensary served chiefly the Christian community in the vicinity. It also acted as an evangelizing agency to some extent to the surrounding Hindu Population.[113] By the end of 1927 Santhapuram Branch Hospital collapsed in a storm. Before the end of 1928, however, this Hospital had been rebuilt on a much larger scale than

---

Telegraph Office and a School in the Marthandam Centre. The spade work done by Emlyn at Marthandam helped for its emergence as a growing centre which still remains as an ongoing process as for as Marthandam is concerned. Marthandam is situated ten miles west of Neyyoor within the borders of Parachalay Mission District. It lies on the main road between Nagercoil and Trivandrum. Formation of the Branch Dispensaries became a regular feature of the Mission throughout the period of the Medical Missionary T.S. Thompson (1873-1884). It is said that this was the last Branch of the Mission Hospital opened during the time of this Medical Missionary (Annual Report of the South Travancore Medical Mission, 1884, 13ff).

108 Annual Report of the South Travancore Medical Mission, 1884, 13.

109 Report of the South Travancore Medical Mission, 1900.

110 Annual Report of the South Travancore Medical Mission, 1926, 10.

111 South Travancore LMS Medical Mission Annual Report, 1922, 10.

112 Martin Daniel Dhas, *Missionary Medical Work in Travancore, 1838-1958*, 122.

113 Report of the Ten years work in connection with the South Travancore Medical. Mission, 1901-1910, 23.

before.[114] Santhapuram was for nearly twenty years a flourishing head-station, but hardly a trace of it is left excepting this Hospital.[115]

Nagercoil was a central place where the Mission had a Branch Hospital. It was put under the charge of Henry, one of the Senior Medical Evangelists.[116] It was this Henry who had built up this work, by attending this Dispensary once or twice a week in addition to his other work.[117] Nagercoil was the rising capital town of the South, principally occupied by a Christian community, but having a large Brahmin Street to the South with Zillah Court at the centre.[118] Further progress of the Nagercoil Hospital required the construction of new buildings.[119] Large male and female wards, smaller rooms for store, etc., had been completed.[120] The amount incurred on the construction at Nagercoil was (about Rs. 3,000) kindly given by Mr. E.D. Pochin. Altogether the work of this Hospital under the supervision of Henry proved a great success.[121] The Dispensary consisted of a simple but neat hall of moderate proportions in which all branches of the work had to be carried out.[122] During these periods the medical missionaries gave special care to lepers and cancer patients. At the same time special concerns were given also to the health care of woman and children. In the time of epidemic the health care units were active in saving the life of the people irrespective of caste, color and creed. Health care training classes were regularly conducted by the medical missionaries to train the native people to assist in the health care mission.

114 LMS Travancore Mission Council Reports and Accounts, 1928, 7.

115 South Travancore Medical Mission Annual Report, 1929, 10.

116 Report of the Ten years work in connection with the South Travancore Medical Mission, 1901-1910, 15-22.

117 Report of the South Travancore Medical Mission for the year 1884, 10.

118 Report of the South Travancore Medical Mission Hospital and Dispensaries for the year 1876, 14.

119 Report of the South Travancore Medical Mission Hospital and Dispensaries for the year 1876, 14.

120 The one hundred and tenth Report of the LMS, 1905, 12.

121 Report of the Ten years work in connection with the South Travancore Medical Mission, 1901-1910, 5.

122 Annual Report of the LMS Medical Mission, 1899, 9.

4. Administrative Growth of Health Care Mission

4.1. Staff of Health Care Mission

The staff position of the Medical Mission at the beginning was shapeless. When it was founded in 1838 its founder was the only staff of the Mission. This position continued for some more time and began to improve with the advent of John Lowe. The staff of the Health Mission under the supervision of John Lowe consisted of a Medical Missionary, a native Health Evangelist and Evangelical Missionary of Neyyoor Mission District.[123] Later a Midwife-cum-Bible Woman[124] also came on to the staff of the Medical Mission.[125] South Travancore Health Mission progressed gradually. Its staff position attained further dimension with the advent of Harlow as its Business Manager.[126] He took care of all the day to day affairs of the Health Care Mission other than the Medical and Surgical care of the patients as well as the matters of male and female nurses.[127]

4.2. Mission Council and the Medical Committee

The Health Care Mission appointed new Doctors and Nurses in accordance with the number of patients coming to the Mission Hospitals. In the beginning they were appointed by the Medical Missionaries. By the turn of events the Medical Committee of the Travancore Mission Council assumed that responsibility.[128] However, the control of the Missionary Staff did not come under the purview

123 Report of the South Travancore Mission Hospital for the year 1869, 11.

124 Bible woman was first appointed to approach the high caste women in their houses to preach the Gospel, to teach them how to write and read in native language and educate them about the fundamentals of health and sanitation as well as to assist them in their child birth in their houses. These Bible woman-cum-midwives were native Christian ladies who were given special course in midwifery from Central Mission Hospital.

125 Report of the South Travancore Mission Hospital and Dispensaries for the year, 1876, 18.

126 London Missionary Society, Ten years of church and Mission in Travancore 1921-30, Nagercoil, 1930, 20.

127 Constitution and Bye-laws of the Travancore Mission Council of the LMS, 1939, 13.

128 Minutes of the Medical Committee, July, 1945.

of the Medical Committee. They were mainly controlled by the Missionaries' Committee of the LMS and approved by the Mission Council and the Medical Committee.[129] In short the ultimate control over the missionaries of the Medical Mission was exercised by the Home Board of the LMS.[130] The Medical Committee appointed non-Christians also as staff of the Health Care Mission. Subsequently, the native Christians gained control over the administration and wanted to monopolize all the positions. In view of that the Medical Committee decided to appoint as far as possible men and women of the LMS congregations as the staff of the Health Care Mission.[131]

4.3. Finance

Finance for the commencement of the LMS Medical work in South Travancore first came from London.[132] Construction of more buildings and the introduction of Medical Courses increased the financial constraints of the Mission. The medical missionaries started a fund called the 'Building Fund' with an amount of one hundred and twenty seven Rupees towards the construction of new buildings for the growing Mission.[133] The Travancore administration encouraged the Medical Mission with an annual grant. Later it was replaced by a monthly maintenance grant in 1920.[134]

The outbreak of the First World War worsened the financial condition of the Mission. To overcome the difficulty Dr. Pugh started the system of charging the patients for medicines, operations and consultations.[135] Business Manager handled the finances of the Health Care Mission. The funding mainly came from the sources of Travancore Government's grant in-aid, patient's offerings, and sale

129 Minutes of the Medical Committee, January - February, 1946.

130 Minutes of the Medical Committee, January - February, 1946.

131 Minutes of the Medical Committee, January - February, 1946.

132 Proceedings of the Travancore District Committee of the LMS Nagercoil, August, 1838, 128.

133 Report of the South Travancore Mission Hospital and Dispensaries for the year 1874, 8.

134 Government of Travancore, General Section File 1-22/29, 1.

135 Annual Report of the South Travancore Medical Mission of the L.M.S. 1921, 47.

of medicines, operations and consultation fees, X-Ray fees, Private Ward rents, Indian Subscriptions, British Subscriptions and the LMS grant.[136]

The foundation of C.S.I. on 27th September 1947 brought remarkable changes in the administration. Since then the South Travancore Diocesan Council of the C.S.I. became the general administrative body instead of the Travancore Mission Council. In a similar manner the Medical Committee was replaced by the Medical Board as the Managing Body of the Health Mission. Based on the Constitution of the Health Mission, financial administration was entrusted to the Treasurer of the Health Mission. He was also a member of the Medical Board duly constituted by the Diocesan Council. This arrangement still continues.[137]

Conclusion

Health care work for of LMS missionaries was really an innovation in the field of health and social service. The arduous efforts of the missionaries could at least indicate the truth that leprosy is a curable disease and at the same time they tried their best to bring lepers back to normal life. Development of the leper asylum from the position of a home to the Hospital proved fruitful to the Society. Patients from all over Travancore and even from neighboring States came to the Mission's Leprosy centre for treatment and consultation. The formation of separate wards to treat the scourge called Cancer with Radium once again happened to be the first of its kind in South Travancore. The Mission gave permanent solution to the problems like the privacy of women. The women's wing of the work organized under the supervision of a female nursing superintendent, attracted large number of women in and around the place to come to the Mission Hospitals for treatment, consultation and child birth. Similarly the X-ray apparatus installed in the Central Hospital also stood as first of its kind in the State. Branch Dispensaries grew into established Christian centers and most of the uncared sections of

136 Travancore Church Council, Statistics and Accounts for 1940, 2.

137 Church of South India, South Travancore Diocesan Council, Constitution and Rules 1947, (Constitution Book) 28.

people embraced the Christian faith. The remedial measures of the Mission during the time of epidemic and diseases such as Cholera and Malaria in the plains and hilly places of the region are note worthy. However, the Health Mission not only saved the life of the people but also it was instrumental in establishing many Churches in South Travancore. The LMS Health Mission made an indelible imprint in the history of the princely state of South Travancore. And also the present day public health systems and health care delivery systems are largely modeled after their approach to medical care.

Chapter 4

Educational Mission in South Travancore (1890 to 1947)

Introduction

Education plays an important role in carving out a healthy and civilized society. It has always been an instrument in bringing out changes in all aspects of the life of people in India. It is true in the case of the people of South Travancore. The Christian missionaries especially LMS missionaries have contributed largely to the educational growth of South Travancore. They started schools, college and various institutions to cater educational benefits to common people in South Travancore. It has helped the people to understand their broken situation and to raise voice for their freedom against oppressive forces. The arrival of missionaries has brought numerous changes in the native education system. The involvement of LMS towards the full-fledged education that offers education up to high school and college levels to the people of South Travancore was immeasurable. Therefore, their tireless efforts in the education sector must be recognized in today's context. In order to understand the role played by LMS in the field of education, one should go into the details of their activities. Hence, this chapter deals briefly with the educational development of the LMS in South Travancore.

1. Education in India

The nature of education in India, then and now, has remained a social and ethical problem. From the *Vedic* times, education has been made the proud possession of only a few privileged groups: the *Brahmins*, *Kshatriyas* and *Vaisyas*. The Sudras and the *Panchamas* were inhumanly excluded from their fundamental right of being educated. The system of education was known as *Dharmashastras,* the particular teaching was done by the upper caste teachers and *gurus* As per the Mahabharata if the low caste allowed then it will be a punishment to upper caste guru because the low caste were not allowed to have education. There were two types of education, one for the rich and middle class, and the other for the poor and low castes.[1]

Schools were functioning in large villages and towns and these schools were controlled by the Hindus and Muslims. Due to the internal disputes and ceaseless wars the prevailed indigenous schools, entirely disappeared.[2] In the 18th century, the native school system was in operation in which there were only three or four classes. The lower ones were under the care and control of the minorities whereas the higher ones were directly under the control of the master who at the same had an eye on the lower ones. This system was very much useful to the upper-caste and they were able to read and learn the religious books, Ramayana, Mahabharata, Panchatantra and the Hindu law were taught in Sanskrit from the earliest period.[3]

The origin of the idea of appropriate female behaviour can be traced to the rules laid down by *Manu*, the law giver in 200 B.C. The condition of woman was dependable, even in her own house .... In childhood, a female must be subject to her father, in youth to her husband, when her husband is dead, to her sons; a woman must never be independent".[4] In the 18th and 19th centuries, the

1 L. Stanislaus SVD, (edit), *Education as Mission,* Ishvani Kendra, ISPCK, Delhi, 2004, 17.

2 P. Subramanian, *Social History of the Tamils*, D. K. Printworld, New Delhi, 1996, 291.

3 P. Subramanian, *Social History of the Tamils*, 292.

4 L. Stanislaus SVD, (edit), *Education as Mission,* 136.

number of educated women was negligible. Education was almost confined to dancing girls because the knowledge of them prescribed and regarded as unbecoming of the modesty of the sex and fit only for public dances. The tradition of the history domestic education was in vogue for women. And the education was made possible only by the Christian missionaries.[5] Government policy to education was not sound enough due to economic and other considerations. The primary education had not seen much improvement in the dawn of 20th century.[6] In the pre-colonial period, the modern missionary movement attempted to offer education as means of social change with the help of Western Education.[7]

1.1. Beginning of English Education

In India for a long time in the past, the presence of the church was mainly by her institutions of modern education, apart from the hospitals and dispensaries. Christian missionaries were the first ones to introduce and institutionalize Western education in India.[8] Western education was critically impartment to social development. It was through education and training that society moulds the human resources for the performance of various tasks.[9] Therefore, after seeing the situations of the people in South Travancore the LMS missionaries evinced keen interest in native education due to various reasons and especially for the purpose of proselytisation.[10]

The pioneers were the Danish missionaries who established religious schools for the instruction of the slaves of the Danish settlement. The Danish missionaries Zigenbalg and Plutschau were the first to impart modern education in and around Tranquebar.

---

5 P. Subramanian, *Social History of the Tamils*, 343.

6 P. Subramanian, *Social History of the Tamils*, 299.

7 Siga Arles, *The Mission of Education: A Comment from India- Where we had been, Where we are, Where we ought to go?*, India Journel of Theology, Vol. XXXXV, 1 / 2, 2003, Accdemy Press, 31.

8 L. Stanislaus SVD, (edit), *Education As Mission,* 15.

9 V. Mathew Kurian, Education as Cultural Transformation, *Church History Review*, Vol. XX1/ 2, December 1997, Church History of Association, Banglore, 90.

10 P. Subramanian, *Social History of the Tamils,* 297.

The work was well recognized by the society and in 1716 they had 21 government approved schools. The LMS missionaries came to Travancore State in 1806 were mainly supported by the Danish Mission. The missionaries followed the education policy of Tranquebar missionaries and began schools to educate the under privileged people of South Travancore. The LMS missionaries were the pioneers of English education in Travancore state, particularly in the South Travancore the area which presently forms the Kanyakumari district. The Protestant missionaries were the first to introduce English education in South Travancore.[11]

The charter of the East India Company in 1813 gave the way for the Christian missionaries to start many schools in their respective mission fields. The charter was interested in introducing useful knowledge and of religious moral improvement.[12] The education system of the LMS was principally composed of three main parts – the Seminary at Nagercoil as the highest institution, the boarding schools and Anglo-vernacular schools as secondary schools, and the village schools as primary schools.[13] The originator of the English school in South Travancore was Rev. William Tobias Ringeltaube (1806), the Christian missionary, who devoted his life to evangelistic work and started many schools for poor children, both Christians and Non-Christians. Another important missionary to be mentioned in connection with the promotion of education is Rev. Mead. The entire credit of establishing the full-fledged educational institutions in the district goes to Rev. Mead and Rev. James Duthie.[14]

The Nagercoil Seminary was established in 1818. It was the first institution to give regular English education in Travancore. Also, until the Maharaja's College was established, it was the head of

---

11 M. Gopalakrishnan. B.Com., *Gazetteers of India. Tamil Nadu Stae*, Kanyakumari District- Madras Printers Industrial Co-Operative Society, Madras, 1995, 841.

12 Siga Arles, *The Mission of Education: A Comment from India- Where we had been, Where we are, Where we ought to go?*, India Journel of Theology, Vol. XXXXV, 1 / 2,31.

13 Koji Kawashima, *Missionaries and a Hindu State Travancore, 1858-1936*, Oxford University Press, Delhi, 1998, 85.

14 Sister A. Mercy, *Kanyakumari District. A Pioneer in Filed of Education*, The New Indian Express. 2nd October, 2000, 12.

educational institutions in South and Central Travancore.[15] There is no doubt that the missionaries regarded their educational activities as an important means of proclamation. Usually the mission schools opened and closed with a prayer, and one hour during the regular school hours was devoted to scripture education.[16] The Seminary was raised to a college in 1893 and became the Scott Christian College.[17] LMS missionaries started girls and boys schools in all most all of their mission fields in south Travancore. The LMS had 141 village schools for boys and 31 for girls in 1861. In these schools, Hindus and children from other communities as well as the LMS Christians were educated.[18] A large number of village schools existed to impart primary education.

From the year 1894 the Travancore government restricted the religious education in aided schools by formulating new educational rules. And the missionaries strongly opposed the new government policy; finally government withdrew its rules.[19] But on 11 June 1904 the order was issued by the government not to continue the religious education in the government aided mission schools and this rule restricted the missionary activities.[20]

2. Development of Educational Mission

Education has always been a primary and privileged mode of the church's mission of preaching the Good News and forming people to become citizens of God's Region.[21] This was very much true with the LMS when the missionary Charles Mead started the seminary and a Central school in the field of education at Nagercoil in 1818, the first institution to give regular English education in Travancore.[22]

---

15 Nagam Aiya, Travancore State Manual, Vol. 11, 446.

16 Travancore District Committee Annual Report, 1868, 10.

17 Occasional Speeches Delivered by Dewan Bahadur M. Krishnan Nair, Dewan of Travancore, 1916 to 1920, Government Press, Trivandrum, 1920, 10.

18 Koji Kawashima, *Missionaries and a Hindu State Travancore, 1858-1936,* 87.

19 Koji Kawashima, *Missionaries and a Hindu State Travancore, 1858-1936,* 105.

20 Koji Kawashima, *Missionaries and a Hindu State Travancore, 1858-1936,* 106.

21 L. Stanislaus SVD, (edit), *Education as Mission,* 15.

22 Nagam Aiya, Travancore Stae Manual Vol. II, 446.

The educational activities of the LMS missionaries attracted the attention of the South Travancore sovereign. In 1836 Swathi Tirunal established free schools for the dissemination of knowledge.[23] But the lower castes were not permitted to attend the government schools and mix with the privileged classes till the last decade of the nineteenth century.[24] The LMS missionaries extended their mission fields. To educate the people, missionaries started schools in all of their mission stations. In the 1860's the LMS had a number of village schools, Separate schools for girls, two boarding schools for boys, three boarding schools for girls and 17 night schools.[25] There was pressure from the people to open schools for all castes. In the 1865 government proposed to establish separate Anglo-Vernacular schools for the children of the Shanars and of such castes as do not mix freely with the Sudras. The missionaries opposed this destructive policy. They were against the principle of imparting knowledge with reference to caste and creed.[26] Another factor that divided the two groups was language. Malayalam was the language of the high caste whereas Tamil was the language of the Nadars and Sambavars. This was a great handicap to the latter in matters of government appointments and the transaction of business with the Government. To make matter worse, the Government began to promote Malayalam by introducing it even in the primary schools of Tamil Taluks and made it compulsory.[27]

One of the important educational institutions of LMS in South India was The Nagercoil Seminary. Till 1862, the studies were carried out chiefly through the medium of the English language. From 1862, it was decided to continue the medium of instruction in English, Malayalam, Tamil and Sanskrit. Each teacher for the seminary was brought from Tranquabar and Tanjore and gradually natives were

23 P. Shungoony Memon, *A History of Travancore*, 145.

24 S. Mateer. Hindu Caste and its Practical Operation, *Indian Evangelical Review*, Vol. 1 October 1872, 228.

25 Dr. S.S. Hector, 'Then Tiruvithankuril Protestant Mission in Samuthya Vallarchi Pannikal' (Tamil), *Bi- Centenary Celebration Year Souvenir 2006*, CSI Diocesan Press, 2006, 154.

26 Koji Kawashima, *Missionaries and a Hindu State Travancore, 1858-1936*, 100.

27 Joy Gnanadhason. *A Forgotten History*, 145.

trained up.[28] James Duthie who was in charge of the institution from 1860 to 1908, obtained the sanction from the Director of LMS to raise funds for a college, affiliated to the University of Madras and was it named Scott Christian College.[29]

The year 1894 was a turning point in the history of education in South Travancore. The government accepted the responsibility for giving education to all classes of people in the state. A new grant-in-aid code was introduced in 1894 to change the educational pattern of the state and the whole educational system was brought under one authority.[30] This measure of the government severely affected the educational work of the LMS missionaries in South Travancore. The government gained the right to interfere in the working of the schools by the introduction of the new code. These regulations prevented the missionaries from using Christian text books, and making their schools a medium for evangelical work. Religions teaching during school hours were strictly forbidden and the missionaries adapted themselves to the new situation by giving religious instruction before school hours.[31] In 1904, it was decided by the government of Travancore to bear the entire cost of the primary education of backward classes and to bear the entire cost of the schools for poor and educationally backward classes.[32]

The order regarding free education to the backward classes of Travancore elicited wide spread approval throughout India. The credit for the establishment of a sound system of education in South Travancore goes to the missionaries of LMS. In 1906, LMS had 140 village schools, 20 girl schools and a college.[33] LMS was not only the

---

28 LMS Yearly Report 1863, 34.

29 LMS Report 1894, 474.

30 LMS Minute Book, 1889-1897, Minutes of the Annual meetings of the Travancore District Council, 280.

31 LMS Yearly Report 1898, 146-147.

32 Travancore Government Gazetteer, Vol. VIII., Travancore Press, 16 August 1904.

33 Dr. S.S. Hector, '*Then* Tiruvithankuril Protestant Mission in Samuthya Vallarchi Pannikal' (Tamil), *Bi- Centenary Celebration Year Souvenir 2006*, CSI Diocesan Press, 2006, 154.

pioneer of English education but also stood as a model for educating the poor sector of the people in South Travancore.

In the year 1893 the Teachers Training School was started by the LMS missionary I.H. Hacker at Marthandam in South Travancore to produce sufficient and qualified trained teachers in the mission schools. But in 1946-1947 Marthandam Teachers Training School and Dathie Teachers Training School were closed because of the financial crisis.[34] When they began their labours in Travancore, the government was least interested in educating the ignorant masses. When the government found that the missionary activities in the educational field were winning laurels, they were inspired to enter the academic area.[35] The government was ready to run the schools therefore the mission board might have given its concern to run the most of the schools established by the missionaries in different mission stations.[36]

The government order shows that 158 mission schools were handed over to the government. And 120 schools buildings were given to government for rent to 12 years. 40 school buildings were used for worship in Sundays and the rest of the days for schools.[37] John Jacob says the handing over process started on 31-05-1946 and finished in the year 1948.[38] However, the mission schools went out from the hand of the missionaries, very few schools were remained and those schools were slowly elevated to the Higher School level. Consequently, they gradually evolved a new educational policy with a view to unite the whole educational system of the State, and the missionary educational institutions were also brought under the control of the government. Thus the missionary educational institutions lost their separate identity.[39]

---

34 G. Christudas, Paathachuvadukal, 206.

35 P. Shungoony Menon, *A History of Travancore*, 414-415.

36 Desopakari, Monthly Magazine, London Mission Press, Nagercoil, Aug, 1945, 15.

37 Government Order 7182 / 1947 on the Primary Schools handing over to the Government.

38 John Jacob, *A History of London Missionary Society in South Travancore*, 221.

39 LMS Yearly Report 1909, 346.

3. Schools for Girls

Before the arrival of the LMS missionaries in the early years of the nineteenth century practically no education was given to women in Travancore as in other parts of India, and their status, compared to men, was very low.[40] Women were considered only as servants to men. India has an ancient and rich tradition of education of women. The Vedic period was the high point, the decline began with the Brahminical forces which imposed restrictions on women's movement, and denied them the right to education. Education of women virtually disappeared in medieval India. During the British period women's education picked up an upward trend, although it was largely due to private initiative till India's independence. In 1901 not even one in a hundred (0.6%) women could read and write.[41] The missionaries wanted to put an end to this state of affairs and improve the status of women by imparting education to them. They thought that the subject of female education was of greatest importance for the future of India. The missionaries of the LMS were the pioneers not only of the Western or English education but also pioneers in the female education in South Travancore. Mrs. Mead and Mrs. Mault, the lady missionaries were the persons who took necessary steps for female education.

A separate school for girls was also started by the missionaries, so as to pave the way for their emancipation. Vocational education also found a place with the starting of a School of Industry. In 1820 they opened a boarding school for the female amidst great opposition from the caste Hindus. In the middle of the 19th century LMS had six boarding schools and thirty one village schools for girls. There was a large extension on female education in the first part of 20th century. Nagam Aiya in 1906 in his book says that "From several centers of missionary activity female education spreads all around and there are, at present, a large number of mission schools".[42]

40 Travancore Administrative Report, 1886 to 1887, 131.

41 L. Stanislaus SVD, (edit), *Education as Mission,* Ishvani Kendra, ISPCK, Delhi, 2004, 136.

42 Nagam Aiya, Travancore State Manual, Vol. 11, 475.

Initially, slaves and orphans were asked to attend school. To meet the daily needs, vocational education was taught by the wife of the respective missionaries. After school hours they taught the girls lace-making, embroidery, crotchet, spinning, etc. The establishment of separate schools for girls was a blessing for the slave girls. Lace making helped them to make out a living. In this way several slave girls became self – reliant and free.[43] In 1921 the LMS at Nagercoil alone employed about 2000 women for its lace industry. All the women were Christians connected with the LMS.[44]

There were no schools for the high caste girls. The prejudice against the education of girls and women were just as strong in south Travancore as elsewhere in India. Though several years had passed since the missionaries started the boarding school at Nagercoil, they had not been able to reach the high caste girls till 1872. The first day school for high caste Hindu girls was opened at Eraniel by Mrs. Thomson. After the year 1882, and a day schools for the high caste girls had been established in Thuckalay, Thiruvithamcode, Thalakulam and Neyyoor.[45] They were taught Tamil, Malayalam, Scripture, Catechism, hymns, Lyric's reading, writing, arithmetic, History of India, Geography, Grammar, Singing, and Needle work.[46] Schools for high caste Hindu girls were opened at Kottar, Vadaseri and Nagercoil. The honour of starting this goes to Rev. Devadason, the first pastor of the Nagercoil Home Church who himself was a Brahmin convert.[47]

Thus the most significant contribution of the wives of the LMS missionaries in south Travancore was their contribution towards girl's education. From the beginning education came to be visibly associated with liberalism. The pioneering work of the missionaries in the field of female education considerably enhanced their status

43 Letter of Mrs. Mault dated Nagercoil 24 June 1930, Indian Evangelical Review, December 1830, I, 540-541.

44 Koji Kawashima, Missionaries and a Hindu State Travancore, *1858-1936,* 98.

45 W.J. Richards, *Twenty Years' CMS in Travancore and Cochin 1858 to 1878*, CMS Press, Kottayam, 1879, 8.

46 Hacker I.H. *A Hundred Years in Travancore, 1806-1906,* 88-89.

47 S.S. Hector, *History of the Church in Kanyakumari Diocese*, (Tamil) Vol. I. 1806-1907, *CSI Dioceson Press, Nagercoil, 1985,* 48.

and opened the eyes of the government to the need of educating the women irrespective of their caste and creed.

4. High School Education

4.1. Ringeltaube Memorials High School, Mylaudy

The LMS schools offered education at different level. For instance, some schools offered only elementary education while others offered up to middle school level. Again some schools offered education up to the high school level. This school started functioning from the year 1908. It was begun by the first missionary of LMS to South Travancore. This school came under Nagercoil mission district. Its campus area is 5 acres. The medium of instruction was Tamil. The total Strength of Ringeltaube Memorial School, Mylaudy was 526 in 1950.[48]

4.2. High School, James Town

This school was established in the year 1814 in Jamestown. Its campus area is 7 acres and consists if building area of 2 acres. In general course Maths, Science and Arts were offered. Tamil was the medium of instruction. Proper laboratory facilities and an auditorium were made available to the students. The sports ground of the school is spread about 3 Acres. Total strength of LMS School, James Town was 436 in 1950.[49]

4.3. Scott Christian High School, Nagercoil

This school was established in the year 1820. In 1867 school was elevated as Matriculation School. In 1873 the school got some government grants. The school was functioning in the place of seminary and this was elevated as a college. Therefore, from 1893 this school was separated and Mr. Paul Daniel served as a head master (1893-1926). He worked hard and in 1898 the school was elevated as High School. In 1899 this school was named as Scott

48 Ten Years Educational Work Report, 1940 to 1950, Ringeltaube Memorials High School, Mylaudy.

49 Ten Years Educational Work Report, 1940 to 1950 Complied from Jamestown Higher Secondary School.

Christian School. It was located at Nagercoil mission district in South Travancore. Its campus area is 7 acres. In general course Maths group, Science group and Arts group and a few vocational courses. The medium of instruction was English and Tamil. The total strength of Scott Christian High School for boy's Nagercoil was 1267 in 1950.[50]

4.4. Dathie High School for Girls, Nagercoil

It was a very old school, established in the year 1821 in the time of Mrs. Johanna Meat and Mrs. Malt. There was no prescribed syllabus before 1873 and the government was able to introduce the syllabus in 1873. In 1930 Hindi was introduced in the schools by the government. From 1938 in Dathie School Hindi was taught to the students. In 1890 the school was elevated to matriculation level.[51] In 1894 Teachers Training School was started by the mission to have more teachers to involve in educational mission. It is located at Nagercoil in Agasteeswaram Taluk. Its Campus area is 10 acres. The school provides Maths, Science and Arts in the general course. The medium of instruction was English and Tamil. In the year 1950 the strength was 2354.[52]

4.5. Girls High School, Neyyoor

This school was established in the year 1828. It is located in the Neyyoor mission district. Its campus area was 12 acres. The general course offers Maths, Science, and Arts. English and Tamil were the medium of instructions. The total strength of LMS Girls School, Neyyoor was 828 in 1950. [53]

50 Ten Years Educational Work Report, 1940 to 1950, Nagercoil. Scott Christian High School.

51 G. Christudas, Pathachuvadukal, 206.

52 Source: Ten Years Educational Work Report, 1940 to 1950, Dathie Girls Higher Secondary School.

53 Ten Years Educational Work Report, 1940 to 1950, Neyyoor Girls Higher Secondary School.

4.6. High School, Kadamalaikuntu

This school was established in the year 1890. This school was located at Neyyoor mission district, functioned as a coeducation school. Its campus area comprises of 7 acres. It general course Maths, Science, and Arts. Tamil was the only medium of instruction. The total strength of this school had been 864 in 1950.[54]

4.7. Girls High School, Marthandam

This school started from 1894. The school comes under the Padasalai mission district. The total area of the school was about five acres. The subjects Maths, Science and Arts were offered as general course in the school. The medium of instruction was Tamil and English. In 1950 the strength was 821.[55]

4.8. High School, South Thamaraikulam

This school was established in the year 1918. It comes under Nagercoil mission district. Its campus area is 5 acres. The subjects Maths Science and Arts are offered at the general level. The medium of instruction was Tamil. In the year 1950 the strength was 812.[56]

4.9. High School, Venkanji

In 1918, this school was established. It is located at Parasalai mission district. Its campus area is 6 acres. The subjects Maths, Science and Arts were offered as the general course. The medium of instruction was Tamil. Proper laboratory facilities and 3 acres of sports ground are available in this school.[57]

---

54 Ten Years Educational Work Report, 1940 to 1950, Kadamalaikuntu Higher Secondary School.

55 Ten Years Educational Work Report, 1940 to 1950, Girls Higher Secondary School.

56 Ten Years Educational Work Report, 1940 to 1950, South Thamaraikulam High School.

57 Ten Years Educational Work Report, 1940 to 1950 Venkanji Higher Secondary School.

4.10. High School, Zionpuram

This school came onto being in 1924. It is located at Nagercoil mission district. Its campus area was 5 acres. Maths, Science and Arts were offered as the general course. The medium of instruction was Tamil. The total strength in the year 1950 was 432.[58]

4.11. High School, Irenepuram

This school started functioning in 1925. It is located at Neyyoor mission district. Its campus area was 7 acres. The subjects Maths, Science and Arts were offered as the general course. The school has both English as well as Tamil as mediums of instruction. The total strength of C.S.I. V.V. School, Irenepuram during the period 1950 was 526.[59]

4.12. High School, Palliyadi

The year of establishment of this school was 1926. It was located at Neyyoor mission district. Its campus area was 6 acres. The general course offers Maths, Science and Arts. The medium of instruction was English and Tamil. The total strength of LMS School, Christucoil, palliyadi was 820 in 1950.[60] During the period of 1890-1947, the said schools were elevated with the government affiliation and financial aid.

5. Health Education

5.1. School of Nursing in Neyyoor

The school of nursing was informally started in 1885. Dr. John Lows established a first medical school at Neyyoor in 1864. Dr. Fry started four to five years health education programme in the year 1889 with 14 students. He followed the Edinburgh health education system and the students were taught Biology, Chemistry, Physiology, Surgery,

58 Ten Years Educational Work Report, 1940 to 1950 Zionpuram Higher Secondary School.

59 Ten Years Educational Work Report, 1940 to 1950, Irenepuram Higher Secondary School.

60 Ten Years Educational Work Report, 1940 to 1950, Palliyadi Higher Secondary School.

Hygiene, Pathology Bacteriology, and Midwifery.[61] Dr. Thomson and others who succeeded him emulated Dr. John Low's plan of training and from 1864 to 1910 six set of young native men were trained at Neyyoor Mission hospital. These trained candidates were known as the dressers or medical evangelist in their working places.[62] They served as assistants to the doctors' in the mission hospitals.

With the arrival of health care missionaries Edith Mills (1926) and Eileen Pidcock (1927), the department of nursing gained a new life. It was in 1923 the formal nursing training was started and the first batch of the students got recognition from the registrar for nursing, Madras in 1926. In the year 1930, the first batch of students under Christian Medical Association of India graduated from this institution. In the same year they started a Training class for higher grade nurses. Men who had passed the E.S.L.C. examination were admitted in nursing school. In the beginning women were not admitted in nursing school. From 1936 the situation changed, and women were admitted for the higher grade nursing course in the nursing school at Neyyoor.[63]

Government recognition for midwifery training was obtained during 1939.[64] Medical mission Neyyoor produced many qualified nurses and they were given opportunity to serve in the mission's health care units. In 1945, Peter a local man trained in Neyyoor School of Nursing, sent to the Christian Medical College, Vellore, for the post gradate training came back and took responsibility for teaching the nurses which had been done so far by missionary nurses alone. In 1946 Miss. Kamalam John joined as the teaching staff in the school of nursing.[65] New leadership was emerging from this time that the local people came forward to concentrate on health care activities. More and more Indian men and women were taken to nursing training and were entrusted with responsibility. LMS medical missionaries imparted the health education to the native people as a

61 G. Christudas, Pathachuvdukal, 166.

62 Joy Gnanadason, *A Forgotten History*, 86.

63 Joy Gnanadason, *A Forgotten History*, 129.

64 M. Gopalakrishnan (editor), Gazetteers of India, Tamilnadu State, 1093.

65 Joy Gnanadason, *A Forgotten History*, 130.

preparation to continue the health mission to save the life of the people of South Travancore from the epidemics and various diseases.

6. College Education

6.1. Scott Christian College

To bring creative leadership in the established churches and institutions, a catechist's theological class was started at Nagercoil in 1885. Few years later the Seminary at Nagercoil was raised to a second-grade college.[66] In 1868 the students studied in the seminary appeared for the matriculation exams. The number of the Christian population was increased and the mission board also began to think of having college level of education for the people of South Travancore. Report was send to the mission body about the need of higher education and the mission board authorized Rev. James Dathi to work for the college education.[67] He got the government permission in 1892. Mr. Denison[68] was send by the mission board to take charge of the college. In the beginning 13 students were admitted for college education (7 Christians and 6 non-Christians).[69] Septimus- Scott[70] liberally contributed for the building construction. To recognize their contributions the Christian college was renamed as Scott Christian College on 31st August 1899.[71]

In 1899 there were 20 students and as per the Indian University Act the Intermediate Course was started in 1904. During the year 1905, there were 37 pupils under instruction and the number rose to

66 I.H. Hacker, *A Hundred Years in Travancore*, 56ff.

67 I. H. Hacker, *A Hundred Years in Travancore,* 57

68 Mr. Denison came to South Travancore on 13-12-1892 and served as a principal of the college for five years from 1894-1899 (G. Christudas, *Paathachuvadukal*, 171).

69 Scott Christian College Student Entry Yearly Report, 1893.

70 Septimus Scott gave Rs. 3,605 in the year 1896 and before the completion of the building work he died then his wife gave Rs. 7,946 to complete the college building work. This family again willfully donated Rs 1000/- for having buildings for Science Block and Library (Mission Report 1899, *Paathachuvadukal*, 172).

71 LMS Mission Yearly Report, 1900, 74.

44 in the very next year.[72] The college admitted students irrespective of caste, colour and creed. The reports of the college show that, from the year 1921 to 1930 there were 37%, and 1930 to 1947 51% Christian students in this college.[73] Girls were not admitted in the beginning. In 1927, G.H. Marsden admitted girls in the college. In 1939 there were about 200 students in this college of whom 20 were women. In the year 1950, the institution was upgraded to the level of a first grade college and degree courses in mathematics (B.Sc) and history (B.A) were started.[74] James Dathi (1893-1894 and 1898-1901), Mr. J.E. Denison (1895-1898), Mr. George Parker (1901-1926), G.H. Marsden (1927-1957) served as the Principals of Scott Christian College.[75]

Conclusion

The ultimate concern of LMS mission was on people's life and their wholistic development. Through education the mission was able to create social awareness among the people. The poor people had no access education. The coming of the LMS missionaries not only made incredible movements in the prevailed educational system that excluded the low caste people but also heralded remarkable changes in the culture of the people. Therefore, it is an undeniable fact that the initiatives taken by the missionaries in the field of education enriched the people with a wealth of human resources that decided their future. They led repeated representations to government about the need of educating the depressed classes and of schools. The relentless educational activities of missionaries to transform the society drew the attention of the government. It also opened the eyes of authorities to give education to all people. Educational opportunities helped the unprivileged classes to advance rapidly in the social scale, and awakened in them a desire for a better life. The educational activities of the missionaries made a perceptible

---

72 Gopalakrishnan (editor) Gazetteers of India, Tamilnadu, State, Kanyakumari District, 867.

73 Scott Christian College Student Entry Yearly Reports, 1899 to 1947.

74 Report from the principal, Scott Christian College, Nagercoil, July, 1989.

75 G. Christudas, Pathachuvdukal, 171.

advancement in the moral and social condition of the backward classes. It is also worth noting that English education played an important role in spreading the gospel of freedom and justice among various language groups. It opened a new vision of political thought and practice in South Travancore along with a realization of a new sense of individuality, dignity and self-respect. The contributions of LMS towards the emancipation of the status of women through education helped the poor women to come up in lives and to be self-reliant in the society. Their efforts not only changed the orthodox tradition of Indian society concerning women but also gave a new social identity to women to lead a dignified life.

Conclusion

The LMS missionaries started their mission activities of South Travancore in a special different socio-religio-economic-political situation. Challenges of the respective context directed the missionaries into various dimensions of societal life. The life-realities of people attracted the attention of missionaries and convinced them of the need of radical changes through education, health care and various community development programmes. As part of their committed efforts to bring changes in the life of people, they opened schools, college, hospital, health care centers, etc. Though the LMS missionaries worked for a long period of one and half centaury, the period of 1890-1947 was remarkable in the history of South Travancore especially in the present Kanyakumari district of Tamilnadu. This period witnessed the upliftment of low caste people mainly in the areas of education and health care that South Travancore society has ever seen before the independence of India.

It can be observed that the activities of LMS in South Travancore in the period of 1890-1947 were done in a political context where British rule was powerful. In South Travancore, native rulers were controlled by the British resident. Socially people were divided on the basis of caste and the low caste people suffered because of the stigma of purity-pollution laws stipulated by high caste people. The high-caste people enjoyed special privileges granted by the local rulers where as the poor low caste people were thrown in to the clutches of various exploitative and oppressive structures. Human dignity and rights of these under privileged people were ignored. Though major religions were existed in the particular period, Hinduism was the prominent faith tradition which discriminated the low caste people through religious customs and practices. Social sanctions made the poor people economically weak and socio-religious regulations kept women inaccessible to education and other community benefits as men enjoyed. In such a context the missionaries initiated drastic steps to make their works effective in the society. They realized that education would change the oppressed condition of the marginalized ones and help them to be more aware of human values. Moreover, the missionaries also understood the need of proper health care for the people who were suffering under epidemics and incurable diseases.

The sacrificial life of missionaries and their families brought educational and health care development in South Travancore. In order to bring the low caste people into the mainstream of society, the LMS mission started higher education. They catered education with a vision of egalitarian society. Because of their timely involvement, the educational system became popular and approachable to all sections of people including the poor and the marginalized. The high caste monopoly on education was broken by the humanitarian face of missionary ventures. Professional education given by the missionaries opened a new way of job opportunities for low-caste people, especially the women. It can also be argued that the missionaries made the government to realize the value of education and motivated the authorities to concentrate more on the education of people. Along with education, the health care mission of LMS also contributed to the development of South Travancore. In the context of the death of thousands of poor workers and women due to the lack of appropriate medical facilities motivated the missionaries to speed up their medical activities. Among them, leper home, cancer ward and maternity wards were appreciated and well recognized both by the people and state. It can be rightly pointed out that these educational and health care contributions were accompanied by the vision of universal humanhood.

The mission endeavors of LMS gave a new momentum to the people who were struggling to affirm their life. The missionaries responded the hopes and aspirations of people with a definitive aim of liberation. In their self-less service, faith has been translated into action. It is also worth noting that LMS mission was always coupled with innovative efforts of community development. In their liberative vision, it not only focused on the issues of people who responded the Gospel but also the entire society irrespective of religious affiliations. It can also be assumed that location and vocation of their ministry was human being and their burning concerns. The determined and concerted mission methods of LMS stand as a role model in the contemporary mission world. The service-minded attempts of LMS remind the present faith community and its supportive organizations to revitalize vision of integral liberation of people in respective contexts. Accommodative method of LMS challenges the Christian community to be more inclusive in their mission endeavors to work for suffering people in the society. The contributions of LMS encourage the Church to re-examine its mission agenda of human liberation. It calls for the faith community to leave 'profit-oriented' mission practices in the society. The mission of Church becomes dynamic when it stands for whole society as LMS labored in South Travancore. Finally, this research comes to the conclusion that the effective involvement of LMS in the educational and health care development in South Travancore was in the period of 1890-1947. This study proposes that further research is needed on the contributions of women missionaries of LMS in South Travancore, the subaltern history of Dalits in South Travancore and the contributions of LMS on the Church Union Movement in South India.

Bibliography

Primary Source

Proceedings of the Travancore District Committee of the LMS, Nagercoil, August, 1838.

Report of the Santhapuram Mission District for the year 1860.

Annual Report of the Neyyoor Mission District, 1860.

LMS Yearly Report, 1863.

Travancore Administrative Report, 1886 to 1887.

LMS Minute Book, 1889-1897, Minutes of the Annual meetings of the Travancore District Council.

Travancore District Committee Annual Report, 1868.

Report of the South Travancore Mission Hospital for the year 1869.

Report of the South Travancore Mission Hospital and Dispensaries for the year 1874.

Annual Report of the South Travancore Medical Mission, 1880.

Annual Report of the South Travancore Medical Mission Hospital and Dispensaries, 1880.

Annual Report of the South Travancore Medical Mission, 1884.

Report of the South Travancore Medical Mission Hospital and Dispensaries for the year 1876.

Scott Christian College Student Entry Yearly Report, 1893.

LMS Yearly Report 1894.

LMS Yearly Report 1898.

Annual Report of the LMS Medical Mission, 1899.

LMS Yearly Report 1909.

Annual Report of the South Travancore LMS Medical Mission, 1897.

Annual Report of the LMS Medical Mission, 1899.

Annual Report of the LMS Medical Mission, 1900.

The one hundred and tenth Report of the LMS, 1905.

Annual Report of the South Travancore Medical Mission, 1906.

Report of the South Travancore Medical Mission, 1908.

Annual Report of the South Travancore Medical Mission, 1908.

Report of the Ten years work in connection with South Travancore Medical Mission, 1901 – 1910.

Report of the South Travancore Medical Mission, 1911.

Annual Report of the South Travancore Medical Mission, 1913.

Travancore LMS Medical Mission Annual Report, 1919.

Annual Report of the South Travancore Medical Mission of the LMS 1921.

South Travancore LMS Medical Mission Annual Report, 1922.

The Hundred and Thirtieth Report of the LMS, 1925.

LMS Report of the Institutional work Industries and properties under the supervision of the Mission council, 1926.

Annual Report of the South Travancore Medical Mission, 1926.

One Hundred and Thirty third Report of the LMS, 1928.

South Travancore Medical Mission Annual Report, 1929.

Annual Report of the South Travancore Medical Mission, 1930.

Annual Report of the South Travancore LMS Medical Mission, 1931.

South Travancore Medical Mission LMS Annual Report, 1933.

Annual Report of the South Travancore Medical Mission, 1938.

LMS Travancore Mission Council Reports and Accounts, 1939.

Constitution and Bye-laws of the Travancore Mission Council of the LMS, 1939.

Travancore Church Council, statistics and Accounts for 1940.

Minutes of the Medical Committee, July, 1945.

Minutes of the Medical Committee, January - February, 1946.

Church of South India, South Travancore Diocesan Council, Constitution and Rules 1947, (Constitution Book).

Annual Meeting of the South Travancore Diocesan Council, 1948.

Government of Travancore, General Section File 1-22/29.

Government Order 7182 / 1947 on the Primary Schools handing over to the Government.

Scott Christian College Student Entry Yearly Reports, 1899 to 1947.

Report from the principal, Scott Christian College, Nagercoil, July, 1989.

Secondary Source

A. H., *Day Dawan in Travancore*, Kottayam: C.M.S. Press, 1860.

Agur, C.M. *Church History of Travancore*. New Delhi: Asian Educational Service, 1990.

Aiya, V., Nagam, *The Travancore State Manual*, Vols. 1 to IV. New Delhi: Asian Educational Services, 1989.

Beaver, R. P., *Ecumenical Beginning of the Protestant World Mission*, New York: Thomas Nelson & Sons, 1962.

Bhatt, S. C., '*Kanyakumari': The Encyclopedic District Gazetteers of India*, Vol. 11. New Delhi : Gyan Publishing House, 1998.

Christdas, G., Paachuvadukal, *History of Church of South India in Kanyakumari Diocese* (Tamil), Palayamkottai: CMS Printing Press, 2005.

Colleridge, James Hendry., *The Life and Letters of St. Francis Xavier, Vol.1*. London: Oxford University Press, 1874.

Daniel, D., *Travancore Tamils Struggle for Identity* 1938–1956, Madurai: Raj Publishers, 1983.

Daniel, Dhas Martin N., *Missionary Medical Work in Travancore, 1838-1958*, Marthandam: South India Press, 1985.

Firth, C. B., *An Introduction to Indian Church History*. Delhi: ISPCK, 1998.

Gladstone, J. W., *Protestant Christianity and People's Movements in Kerala, 1850-1936.* Trivandrum: The Seminary Publications, KUTC, 1984.

Gnanadason, Joy., *A Forgotten History: The Story of the Missionary Movement and the Liberation People in South Travancore*, Madras: GLTC, 1994.

Gopalakrishnan, M. (Ed)., *Gazetteers of India, Tamilnadu State, Kanyakumari District.* Madras: Printers Industrial Co-operative Society, 1995.

Goodall, Norman., *A History of the London Missionary Society, 1895-1945*, London: Oxford University Press, 1954.

Hacker, I. H., *A Hundred Years in Travancore*, A Centenary Memorial Volume of the Work of the London Missionary Society, South India. London: H. R. Allenson Limited, 1908.

Hector, S.S., *History of the Church, Kanyakumari Diocese 1806 to 1907*, Vol. 1 (Tamil), Nagercoil: Diocesan Press, 1970.

Hoefer, Herbert., *Debate on Mission*, Chennai: Gurukul Lutheran Theological and Research Institute, 1979.

Jacob, A John., *A History of the London Missionary Society in South Travancore, 1806-1959,* Nagercoil: The Diocesan Press, 1990.

_______ *Triple Jubilee Commemoration Volume 20th Aug, 1956*, Nagercoil: London Mission Press, 1956.

Jeyakumar, D. Arthur., *History of Christianity in India- Selected Themes*, Madurai: Tamilnadu Theological Seminary, 2000.

Joy, Hepzy R.J., *History and Development of Education of Women in Kerala,* Trivandrum: KUTS, Seminary Publication, 1995.

Kawashima, Koji., *Missionaries and a Hindu State of Travancore, 1858-1936*, Delhi: Oxford University Press, 1998.

Kooiman, Dick., *Conversion and Social Equality in India*, New Delhi: Manohar Publishers, 1989.

Kumaradoss, Vicent K., *Robert Caldwell, A Scholar-Missionary in Colonial South India*, Delhi: ISPCK, 2007.

Kuriakose, M. K., *History of Christianity in India: Source Materials*, Delhi: ISPCK, 1982.

Latourette, K. S., *A History of Expansion of Christianity*, Vol, IV. New York: Harper & Brothers Publishers, 1944.

Mateer, Samuel. *Native Life in Travancore,* London: London Mission Press, 1883,

_______., *The Land of Charity*, London: John Snow and Company, 1871.

Menon, A. Sreedhara, *A Survey of Kerala History*, Kottayam: National Book Stall, 1970.

Menon, A. Sreedhara., A *Survey of Kerala History*, New Delhi: 1980.

Menon, K. P. Padmanabha., *History of Kerala*, Vol. 11. Ernakulam: Cochin Government Press, 1929.

_______ *History of Kerala*, Vol. 111. edited by T.K. Krishna Menon, New Delhi: Asian Educational Services, 1993.

Menon, P. Shanoony., *A History of Travancore from the Earlier Times*, Madras: Higginbotham and Co, 1887.

Mohammed, V. Jamal., *"Kerala", in Dravidian Encyclopedia,* edited by Subramanian, Vol. II, Thiruvananthapuram: The International School of Dravidian Linguistic, 1993.

Neill, Stephen., *A History of Christianity in India: The Beginning to AD 1707*, Cambridge: Cambridge University Press, 1984.

Owen, White House John., *Register of Missionaries Deputations*, London: London Missionary Society, 1896.

Paul, R. D., *Neelakandan Devadasan*. Madras: CLS, 1971.

_______ *Triumphs of His Grace*, Madras: CLS, 1967.

Pillai, P.N. Kunjan., *Studies in Kerala History*, Kottayam: National Book Stall, 1970.

Pillai, T.K. Velu., *The Travancore State Manual*, Vols. 1 to IV Trivandrum: Travancore Press, 1940.

Powl, Bethval., *Visvasathin Sathanai, C.S.I. Varalattu Pinnani*, (Tamil), Chennai: Thiruchabaikalin Samaya Kalvikuzu, 1996.

Richards, W.J., *Twenty Years' CMS in Travancore and Cochin 1858 to 1878*, Kottayam: CMS Press, 1879.

Robert, Caldwell., *Records of the Early History of the Tirunelveli Mission of the SPCK and SPG*, Madras: Higginbotha & Co, 1881.

Robinson, William., *Ringeltaube, the Rishi*, Sheffield: The Sheffield Independent Press Ltd, 1902.

Schoff, Philip., *Religious Encyclopedia of Dictionary, Biblical, Historical, Doctrinal, and Practical Theology*, Vol. 11, Edinburgh T &T Clark, 1883.

Sherring, M.A., *The History of Protestant Missions in India: From their Commencement in 1706 to 1881,* London: The Religious Tract Society, 1884.

Soares, Aloysius., *Catholic Church in India: A Historical Sketch*, Nagpur: Government Press and Book Depot, 1964.

Sobanan, B., *A History of the Christian Mission in South India*, Trivandrum: Manju Publishing House, 1996.

Somervell, T. Howard., *Knife and Life in India: The Story of a Surgical Missionary at Neyyoor, Travancore*, London: The Living Stone Press, 1955.

Stanislaus, L. (ed.)., *Education as Mission*, Delhi : Ishvani Kendra, ISPCK, 2004.

Subramanian, P., *Social History of the Tamils*, New Delhi: D. K. Printworld, 1996.

Tekkadeth, Joseph., *History of Christianity in India*, Vol.1, Bangalore: CHAI, 1982.

Thayalan, Prabavathi. *Pioneer Missionaries of Marthandam and Parasalai* (Tamil), Nagercoil: Tower Grafics Printers, 2000.

Travancore Government Gazetteer. Vol. VIII, Travancore Press, 16 August 1904.

Trivandrum : Travancore Government Press, 1920.

Vedanayagamoni, Peter., *Introduction to History of Christianity in India*, Chennai: Hindustan Bible Institute, 1989.

Verkuyl, Johannes., *Contemporary Missiology*, Michigan: William B. Eerdmans Publishing Company, 1975.

Western, F. J., *The Early History of the Tinnevelly Church*, London: Oxford University Press, 1938.

Yesudas, R.N., *A People's Revolt in Travancore: A Background Movement for Social Freedom,* Trivandrum: Kerala Historical Society, Manju Publishing House, 1975.

_______ *British Policy in Travancore*, Trivandrum: Kerala Historical Society, Manju Publishing House, 1977.

Zachariah, Samuel., *A Summery of the History of the Church in South Travancore1805-1855*(Tamil), Vol. I, Nagercoil: LMS Mission Press, 1897.

_______ *A Summery of the History of the Church in South Travancore, 1855-1906*, (Tamil), Vol. 11, Nagercoil: LMS Press, 1906.

Articles in Edited Volumes

Christdhas, D., "A Short History of the C.P. Memorial Leprosy Hospital" *Leprosy Hospital's Jubilee Souvenior* Nagercoil: LMS Press, 1940, pp 140-180.

Dathie, James., "Education", *Desaupakari, LMS's Monthly Magazine* Nagercoil: LMS Press, 1945, pp 9-14.

Edmunds, Thomas., "Tranquebar Missionaries and Three- Hundred Years of Lutheran Heritage: An Analysis," *Tercentenary Souvenir, Tamil Evangelical Lutheran Church,* Tiruchirappalli, Best Offset, 2006, pp 14-26.

Hector, S.S., " Then Tiruvithankuril Protestant Missionin Samuthya Vallarchi Pannikal", (Tamil), *Bi-Centenary Celebration Year Souvenir 2006,* CSI Diocesan Press, 2006, pp 154-157.

Joyal, Selin., "Cancer Patient," *Desaupakari, CSI Kanyakumari Diocese*, February, 2008, pp 13-16.

Mathew, K.M., "Religious Life of the Travancore", *Manorama Year Book, "History of Kerala, 27th Year of Publication"*, Malayala Manorama, Kottayam- Kerala, 1992, pp 17-23.

Padmanabhan, S., "Historic Churches in Kanyakumari, Vol. V *Aayvu Kalanjiam, Nagercoil,* December 2003, pp 36-40.

Articles in Journals

Arles, Siga. "The Mission of Education: A Comment from India- Where we had been, Where we are, Where we ought to go?" *India*

Journal of Theology, Vol. XXXXV No1&2, (June 2003): Academy Press, pp. 30-40.

Gladstone, J.W. "19th Century Mass Movement in South Travancore- A Result of Social Liberation." *Indian Church History Review*, Vol. X No. 1, (June 1976): pp 53-66.

Kooiman, Dick. "Social and Economic Backgrounds of 19th Century London Missionary Society in South Travancore", *Indian Church History Review*, Vol. XIX No. 2, (December 1985): pp 99-127.

Kumar, Suresh John. "Christian Medical Care in Tamil Nadu." *Indian Church History Review,* Vol. XXXV11 No. 2, (December 2003): pp 91-108.

Kurian, Mathew V. "Education as Cultural Transformation." *Indian Church History Review*, Vol. XXI No. 2, (December 1997): pp. 90-103.

Mateer, S. "Hindu Caste and its Practical Operation", *Indian Evangelical Review*, Vol. 1 (October, 1872): pp. 228-234.

Mault. "Letter to Mission Society dated Nagercoil 24 June 1930", *Indian Evangelical Review,* (December-1830): pp. 40-47.

Manickam, Raja. "S. Robert de Nobili and Adaptation," Indian *Church History Review*, Vol. 1 No. 2, (December 1967): pp. 83-91.

Sathianesan, V. "Reconversion Impulse in Travancore." *Indian Church History Review,* Vol. XXVI No.1, (June 1992): pp. 5-20.

Sharma, M. K. "Nair Women of Kerala", *Dalit Voice*, Vol. 7, No. 23, (October, 2005): pp. 16-31.

Suneja, Alin. "Letters of St. Francis Xavier as a Source for 16th Tamilagam," *Indian Church History Review,* Vol. XXXV No. 1, (June 2001): pp. 62-75.

Daily News and Unpublished Sources

The New Indian Express, 5th May, 1999, 7

The New Indian Express, 2nd October, 2000, 6

Jebanesan, M. Jezer., "As a Movement of Liberation of the oppressed in South Travancore", a paper presentation in an International

Seminar on Bearing Witness to the God made known in Christ in India Today at Peace Trust Kanyakumari on 23rd August 2006.

Krishnan, Nair Dewan and M. Bahadur., *Dewan's Occasional Speeches* 1916 to 1920.

Samuel Bhanu, "Vedamanikam", (B.D. Thesis, Gurukul Lutheran Theological College and Research Institute, Chennai, 1997).

Ten Years Educational Work Report, 1940-1950, LMS High Schools.